CW00742494

THE SUBMARINE
COMMANDER
POCKET MANUAL 1939–1945

Edited by Chris McNab

CASEMATE
Oxford & Philadelphia

Published in Great Britain and
the United States of America in 2018 by
CASEMATE PUBLISHERS
The Old Music Hall, 106–108 Cowley Road, Oxford OX4 1JE, UK
1950 Lawrence Road, Havertown, PA 19083, USA

Introduction and chapter introductory texts by Chris McNab
© Casemate Publishers 2018

Hardback Edition: ISBN 978-1-61200-655-0
Digital Edition: ISBN 978-1-61200-656-7

A CIP record for this book is available from the British Library

Printed and bound in the United Kingdom by TJ International

The information and advice contained in the documents in this book is solely for
historical interest and does not constitute advice. The publisher accepts no liability for the
consequences of following any of the advice in this book.

For a complete list of Casemate titles, please contact:

CASEMATE PUBLISHERS (UK)
Telephone (01865) 241249
Fax (01865) 794449
Email: casemate-uk@casematepublishers.co.uk
www.casematepublishers.co.uk

CASEMATE PUBLISHERS (US)
Telephone (610) 853-9131
Fax (610) 853-9146
Email: casemate@casematepublishers.com
www.casematepublishers.com

Cover design by Katie Gabriel Allen

CONTENTS

INTRODUCTION

It is relatively rare in warfare for individual weapon systems to have a truly important *strategic* (as opposed to tactical) effect on a conflict, yet the submarine can justifiably make such a claim. From its crude beginnings in the 18th century, and its early haphazard forays into combat during the American Civil War (1861–65), the submarine became a potentially war-winning instrument by the early 20th century. This jump forward came courtesy of several major technological innovations all coming into alignment, not least the development of all-metal hull construction (giving a properly watertight hull), invention of the self-propelled torpedo by Robert Whitehead in the 1860s and 1870s, and the replacement of steam propulsion (never truly practical for submarines) with diesel internal combustion engines for surface running and electrical batteries for submerged running. With some impractical exceptions, the submarines that emerged by 1914 were a fraction of the size and complement of large surface warships, yet had the capability of killing even the greatest of battleships, and doing so while remaining unnervingly hidden and largely silent below the waters.

The strategic potential of the submarine became apparent, brutally so, during World War I. As an early indicator of their power, on 22 September 1914 the German submarine *U-9*, captained by Otto Weddigen, encountered three British armoured cruisers – HMS *Aboukir*, HMS *Hogue* and HMS *Cressy* – in the southern North Sea, and promptly sank all of them in less than an hour, with the loss of 62 officers and 1,397 men. It was shocking proof of the submarine threat, and throughout the war and into the next global conflict, just the presence, real or imagined, of enemy submarines had a profound restrictive effect on the willingness to deploy major surface combat warships.

Yet it was when applied to attacking merchant shipping that the full strategic potential of the submarine became apparent. Again, Germany was a pioneer in this matter, largely because one of its principal foes – Britain – was a maritime nation fundamentally dependent upon shipborne logistics. Especially from the introduction of unrestricted German submarine warfare in February 1917, the rates at which merchantmen were destroyed rose to astonishing levels. In April 1917 alone, one in every four British merchant vessels heading for a British port from across the Atlantic was sunk. By war's end, more than 13 million tons of British (or Britain-bound) shipping had been sunk, expressed in the cost of more than 2,000 ships and 14,000 lives. Had it not been for wider strategic developments, not least the fact than the German submarine campaign helped to bring the United States into the war, Britain could potentially have been starved into submission.

During the inter-war years, the lessons concerning the efficacy of submarines were not lost on the world powers. The United States, United Kingdom, France, Japan, Russia and Italy all invested heavily in the numbers and types of submarines. German was technically stripped of all its submarines under the terms of the Versailles Treaty, although it kept U-boat research alive through proxy agencies in the Netherlands, Spain and the USSR, research that was jump-started into production vessels once the Nazis came to power in 1933. The inter-war developments were not always coherent or considered, with many navies uncertain about whether to lean their investment towards smaller coastal submarine types or larger ocean-going specimens. Yet once war began in 1939, it became quickly apparent that the open-water submarine would have an even greater potential impact than it had in the previous global war.

At sea, World War II was a conflict arguably defined by the submarine, even more so than that other seminal naval innovation of the war, the aircraft carrier. The depredations of the U-boats in the Atlantic theatre are particularly well known. Once the French Atlantic ports were in German hands from mid-1940, giving the U-boats easy access to the trans-Atlantic sea lanes, the killing of Allied Atlantic shipping rose to terrifying levels – 3.65 million tons in 1940 (1,007 ships), 3.29 million tons (875 ships) in 1941, 6.15 million tons (1,170 ships in 1942) and 2.17 million tons (363 ships) in 1944. Once again, Britain was under the shadow of potential starvation; as the redoubtable Winston Churchill admitted in 1949 memoirs, "The only thing that ever really frightened me during the war was the U-boat peril."

But we should not let the Atlantic theatre overshadow the intensity of submarine actions elsewhere. Britain's Submarine Service, for example, conducted a withering submarine campaign in the Mediterranean against mainly Italian shipping attempting to run supplies to Axis forces in North Africa. Russian submarines preyed on German vessels in the Baltic, especially during the last two apocalyptic years of the war. In the Pacific theatre, submarine warfare was every bit as strategically significant — if not more so — than in the Atlantic. Japan's own submarine campaign was vigorous, and its victims included several US aircraft carriers, escort carriers and battleships amongst more than 42 total kills. Here, however, was the root cause of Japan's failure to use its submarines more persuasively. The Japanese high command continually insisted on using submarines to target warships, rather than the merchant shipping that was critical to the entire US Pacific campaign. The Americans, by contrast, embraced war against Japanese merchant shipping with unbridled ferocity. In fact, Japan began the Pacific War with 2,337 merchant vessels, but by the end of the war had just 231 left, most of the fleet being sent to the bottom by US submarines. The effect on a country almost entirely dependent on maritime means for its supply of raw materials was utterly crippling, and underpinned the Japanese defeat as much as any other cause.

Yet the picture we have painted so far neglects one key fact — serving in a submarine was one of the most dangerous military professions imaginable. As much as submarine technology improved, anti-submarine weapons and tactics kept pace, or in some theatres exceeded the submarine's defences. This reality was most horrifically visible in the Atlantic theatre, where by 1944 the life expectancy of a U-boat crew had dropped to around 100 days. In 1940, just 23 U-boats were sunk, but by 1943 the annual losses rose to 237 submarines, and 242 the next year. Although such kill rates were exceptional during the war, the fact was that serving on submarines was a dangerous business indeed, and one that therefore drew upon a unique breed of men.

In 1941, during some of the darkest days of the British war, a Professor A. M. Low published a book entitled *The Submarine at War*. This volume not only charted the history of undersea warfare, but more important, it laid out the qualities of the men who crewed the submarines, and the extreme nature of the physical and psychological challenges they faced. Professor Low seemed particularly motivated by two causes: first, to give the largely hidden but heroic work of the Submarine Service a higher public profile; second, to dispel any myths about the glamour of what the crews were called upon to do. The following passage, taken from Chapter 6 "The Men in the 'Trade'", gives a flavour of Low's sincere reflections:

How do the men in a submarine spend their time? Sleeping, reading, eating, and working. They sleep more than most men when on patrol, partly perhaps out of boredom, partly because there is no possibility of much movement in the submarine and "lying down" is the most comfortable position. They are ready, of course, for instant action at any time and turn straight from their beds to duty; as a rule they have only a pace or two to go. Conditions in modern submarines are infinitely better than in the little A, B, and C class boats; there is no doubt that increased comforts, although these are only comparative, make for greater efficiency and longer cruises. The conditions are quite unlike those of any other boat, for here you have from 30 to 60 men enclosed in a small space with no possibility of getting away from each other even if they wanted to do so. The absence of daylight means that one day slips into another and time moves at varying speeds. Another interesting point is the silence when the submarine submerged. In most parts of the boat only the faint hum of the motor can be heard when it is turning, and for hours the boat may simply rest on the bottom without making any sound at all.

The crew of the submarine are in the most dangerous trade in the world; the Navy sometimes calls the submarine service "the trade." At the time of writing, during the "Axis" war, the loss has been announced of some twenty-two British submarines. Britain began the war with fifty-eight submarines. This is a measure of the hazards of the service, more dangerous, perhaps, than

A game of cards and a smoke alongside the torpedo tubes of a British submarine.

even torpedo-aircraft. The submarine has been a dangerous vessel from the beginning, at first because of the inefficiency and uncertainty of its controls, later because of the improved methods of attack to which it is subject. These methods have been still further improved since the Great War; the Germans lost more U-boats in the first 10 months of the 1939 war than in any year of the great war from 1914 to 1918.

Bearing this in mind it is remarkable that there had never been lacking volunteers for submarines; the service is entirely voluntary. It is a curious fact that in civilised countries all the more dangerous jobs are voluntary. The submarine crew does not, moreover, enjoy any of the physical exhilaration experienced by the pilot of a fighter aircraft; in most cases only one of the whole crew will ever see the target which is being attacked. Even if there were no danger attached the work it is most exhausting because of the physical conditions imposed by a closed vessel operating underwater. These facts apply equally to the submarine crews of Germany has to Britain.

This passage has been quoted at length because in many ways it perfectly captures the universal experience of submarine operations during World War II, and the distinct experience of the men who crewed these specialised vessels. All military personnel in wartime are familiar with boredom, deadening routines and long periods of inactivity. For submarine crews, however, such tedious states of being were taken to the limits of human endurance, and within an unforgiving operating environment.

For a start, there was the issue of confinement. Anyone who suffered from genuine claustrophobia was weeded out during the selection process, but all those who manned submarines had to adjust to the most compressed living and working space. The German Type VIIB submarine, for example, was one of the most important of the German types at the beginning of World War II. It had a length of 218ft 3in (66.52m) and a beam of 20ft 3in (6.17m), typical of many medium-sized submarines used in the war. Within this craft served 44 men; if the crew stood side by side along the full length of the submarine, this would equate to just under 5ft (1.5m) of room for each individual. Yet in reality, the crew lived and worked inside the far smaller inner pressure hull space, which was in turn packed with equipment and stores. (Submarines typically consist of two hulls, an outer hull that provides the submarine's hydrodynamic outer shape and an inner pressure hull that resists the pressure of seawater when the submarine is submerged, and which contains all the living and working spaces for the crew.) With space at such an acute premium, the crew almost literally lived on top of one another, with privacy of any sort impossible to achieve. Bunks were strung up in any available space (especially in the quieter torpedo rooms); even so, many crew members were compelled to "hot bunk", only sleeping in a bunk when it was vacated by another man on duty. Because of the need to cram the submarine with enough supplies for 2–3 months of self-sustained operations at sea, actual space for personal effects per man was typically in the region of just 1ft (0.3m) cubed.

Added to this compression of humans into limited physical space was a grim litany of physical effects. Because of the very limited availability of fresh water, washing (body or clothes) and shaving were rare or absent occurrences, resulting in skin diseases and rancid air, the smell of body odour and aggressive deodorants mixing with those of toilet compartments, rotting vegetables, salt water, diesel fuel and engine oil. Temperatures inside the submarine reached equatorial levels, especially when the boat was submerged, resulting in heavy sweating into clothes that would not be changed for weeks. Even when the submarine was cruising on the surface, the ability to rotate crew out on to deck for a literal breath of fresh air was limited for both safety and practical reasons – there was typically only one small point of entrance and egress, via the conning tower. Over the space of several weeks, the crew member might spend only a few hours gulping down fresh air. All work inside the submarine was conducted by garish electric light, so not only could fresh air be a rarity, but daylight was also effectively rationed. Food quickly became repetitive, especially when the submarine had not visited a friendly port for many weeks, and fresh produce had long perished. The lack of daylight, fresh air, fresh fruit and vegetables produced men with grey, washed-out skin of the most unhealthy pallor.

The size and type of submarines varied considerably within and between the combatant navies. As a general rule, the submarine crews of the US vessels, and some of the larger Japanese types, had the most space and comfort, but "comfort" was strictly relative, especially over the duration of operational cruises that might last up to six months, or even longer. Most of this time would be spent either warily cruising across endless miles of featureless ocean, or periodic underwater manoeuvres, down to depths of up to – and in emergency exceeding – some 656ft (200m).

To this picture of general submarine life, we add the occasional thrill and terror – the two typically went hand-in-hand – of combat. All that separated the crew from violent death was a few millimetres thickness of steel. The submarine hull, already under tons of water pressure, could be subjected to the proximate and repeated detonations of enemy depth charges, which inflicted their damage via thunderous primary and secondary shock waves rippling out through the incompressible water. Any depth charge that exploded within 33ft (10m) of the submarine hull would hurt the vessel, or the crew inside, who were thrown around like swaying puppets against the unyielding metal surfaces. If the depth charge detonated within 13ft (4m), then the result would likely be a catastrophic hull failure. Sea water would roar through the ship with an explosive rush and drown the entire crew, or at least flood a portion of the ship and send the vessel to the bottom of the sea, unable to raise itself. There the crew would remain, sometimes able to escape, but often consigned to an unimaginable collective end through slow oxygen starvation. New weapons, such as impact-detonated pattern depth charges like the Allied "Hedgehog" and the escalating threat of sudden air attack from specialised anti-submarine aircraft, meant that there were few times at sea when a crew felt safe. In return, they visited their own brand of destruction

Central control. While the captain keeps watch through his periscope, the men keep their stations for all the while the submarine is submerged.

upon the enemy, the tension of weeks of furtive patrolling finally released in the audible boom of a torpedo striking the underside of a ship's hull.

Holding this dark world together was the submarine's captain. Such individuals were almost uniformly impressive, in their force of personality (quiet or otherwise), their intelligence and their ability to inspire and motivate their crew. They were in a uniquely intimate command relationship with their men, knowing almost every individual personally, yet having to strike the right balance between strict discipline – on which a submarine utterly depends – and more informal leadership. Again Professor Low captures this picture perfectly:

> The officers and crew are thrown together for the whole of their waking and sleeping time which makes for a comradeship that would not arise under other conditions. Button-polishing and all it represents is completely absent. Officers and men alike are often unshaved for lack of water. Yet discipline in its finest sense is even more necessary than in any other service, for on the unquestioning carrying out of orders depends the safety of the ship. The men must have implicit faith in their commander; he alone, his eyes on the periscope, can see what is happening. And he in his turn must have implicit faith in his juniors and crew so that he can concentrate. Very real concentration is required to navigate the ship, plan an attack and avoid being caught unawares all at the same time without being disturbed by the thought that orders may not be carried out properly. This very difficult combination of comradeship and discipline is, in fact, developed by the peculiar conditions of the service. Nowhere have officers greater respect for their men.

This book brings together excerpts from official submarine publications produced during or in the very immediate aftermath of World War II. They come from a variety of sources – British, American and German – but all of them convey the same impression of the vast range of demands a submarine commander had to understand and embrace. He had to have all the technical knowledge of an engineer, the man-management skills of a psychologist, the emotional presence of the leader, the ruthless cunning of a hunter, and the watchful caution of prey. Not all of the manuals given here were exclusively focused on educating the commander himself, but would also have been digested by various other members of the crew. Yet one key distinguishing factor about submarine service was that each man, including the commander, had to some degree understand how to perform the duties of the other men on the craft. Truly the submarine was a community of men at war.

CHAPTER I
TRAINING AND CREW ROLES

An official British government publication, *His Majesty's Submarines* was published in early 1945, its main purposes being to educate the general public about life aboard a submarine but also to give background information to those thinking of joining the Submarine Service. This small booklet provided a potted history of British submarine campaigns up to the end of 1944, but it also gave an insight into the nature of the crew, their roles and responsibilities, and their experience at sea. In most of the world's navies, submarines were largely manned by volunteers, men attracted towards the unusual technical and tactical characteristics of submarine warfare. This volunteer status bred an e*sprit de corps* and the sense of being a small elite within a larger navy. The exigencies of war, however, could change the recruitment pool of personnel. In Germany, for example, the U-boats were for at least the first three years of the war manned almost exclusively by enthusiastic volunteers, attracted by the public veneration of the submariners, who were depicted frequently in magazines such a *Signal!*, plus the apparent operational freedom of the submarine. Yet by late 1943 the pool of volunteers, especially in skilled engineering professions, was becoming constrained as the poor life expectancy of U-boat crews became apparent. Thus we find some men being diverted from non-naval professions into the submarines, being "invited" to join the submarine arm and complying through exerted moral pressure. But the submarines largely remained the preserve of open and willing volunteers, generally from within the merchant of military navies. Depending on the level of skill they brought with them, a basic training period of 4–6 weeks would precede deployment to an operational submarine, the young crewman learning the rest of his skills on the job.

His Majesty's Submarines (1945)

The submarine moved slowly at periscope depth. In the control room the captain, standing at the periscope, watched the empty Mediterranean. The conditions on that December day were perfect for an attack. A fresh wind made the white horses leap in the bright sunlight. In the eyepieces glowed the reflected blue of sea and sky as the captain turned the periscope and followed the unrelieved horizon round.

He knew how perfect conditions were, how seldom there was enough wind to hide the plume of water thrown up by the periscope, and how often the periscopes feather was the only great in the flat surface of the sea. Now there lacked only a target. The captain paused? to tear off a shred of tissue paper and wipe the moisture from the lenses. Again, with head and shoulders bent forward, he turned the periscope.

"Ah, here we are."

In the control room the diving watch on duty had the quiet, casual words.

"Yes, this is it – two of 'em – oh, lovely, lovely. Down periscope."

With a hiss, the periscope moved downwards until its lower end had disappeared into the well that housed it. All hands closed up at action stations; the torpedo tubes were brought to the ready; the attack team grouped themselves around the captain. There was silence again.

"Up periscope."

The captain crouched almost to his knees to seize the handles and put his eyes to the instrument; it rose slowly till the upper window reappeared in the sunshine. He looked for a second time at the target and in the same unhurried manner called out the attack data – bearing, angle on the bow, range. The attack had begun.

Days later, after the submarine's return, the Captain (S) – the officer commanding the submarine flotilla – received the narrative of the attack.

1240 Sighted two supply ships approaching on a course for Bizerta. Two ships later seen to be one supply ship of about 4,000 tons, and one medium-sized tanker, disposed in line abreast, with two T.Bs. (torpedo boats) on either bow as escort. Unfortunately the tanker was on the far side from the submarine, and the other vessel had to be the target.

1330   In position 38° 20′ N., 12° 35′ E. Fired four torpedoes.

1332^1/$_2$ Two explosions at an interval corresponding to that between the first and second torpedoes.

1334   One explosion 1 minute 15 seconds after the second hit. This may have been the first depth-charge, or possibly a hit on the tanker, which at the time of firing appeared to be one ship's length astern of the supply ship. The submarine proceeded towards the enemy's stern.

1336   Depth-charges dropped singly. This was followed by a pair of depth-charges, and then another single one at about 2-minute intervals. The counter attack was carried out by one T.B. using asdic. A pattern of 10, dropping fairly close, shook the submarine, causing no damage.

1406   T.B.'s screw heard passing overhead, very slowly.

1406^1/$_2$ A pattern of 12 charges dropped close, causing showers of cork, though it caused little real damage beyond lights being smashed and a few small leaks. It is considered that this pattern was dropped slightly on the port quarter and was fortunately set too shallow. After this that patterns became more distant, but, no matter what alterations of course were made, the enemy could not be shaken off.

About 1700 another T.B. joined in the hunt, unfortunately seem to hinder rather than help his expert consort, as only three charges were dropped after this time, although one T.B. was hurt passing overhead.

At 1830 all H.E. (hydrophone effects) had ceased. 62 charges had been dropped in the counter-attack.

2008   Surfaced. Withdrew to N.E. Subsequently setting course to Malta, all torpedoes being expended.

In such simple words of pages written in the history of submarines, in the history of war. The narrative is of bare fact, and one of many hundreds which have been written by the commanding officers of His Majesty's submarines since the morning of 3rd September 1939.

This patrol report was read carefully by Captain (S), for he was responsible for the organisation and maintenance of the flotilla, and for planning, in accordance with the strategy of the war, the details of each patrol. It was his unenviable duty to send younger men into danger when he would have preferred to go himself, to give orders and to wait, perhaps four weeks, for word of their fulfilment. But on this patrol all had gone well, and, the success having been confirmed, he could remark: "This was a very valuable patrol, carried out with fine dash and judgement, which cost the enemy two ships full of water supplies."

The road to the sea. The submarine slips down the estuary in the evening light. She goes alone, with few to watch her. Only the men of her depot ship and of the submarines still secured alongside are there to wonder how she will fare.

An attack by a submarine may take only a few minutes, but the moment when the word "Fire" lights on the order instrument at the fore ends and the torpedo is released is the climax of many years of preparation. The success of an attack depends on more than the nicety of a captain's judgement; it depends on the shipbuilder's skill, on research and experiment in peace and war, on a long succession of ordeals and triumphs, and, above all, on courage and resolution.
[. . .]

Submarine Captain

There is no typical submarine captain. Here and there among them is an inheritor of the Elizabethan tradition, whose bearded face and individual ways give colour to his character, who flavours his deeds and words with a taste from his own personality so that they are passed from mouth to mouth until they form a legend around his name. But there are many others who lacks such outward characteristics, who would pass unnoticed in a crowd, except perhaps for a row of medal ribbons unusually long, and whose manner is quiet and unassuming. They are not less skilled or fearless. They approach the specialised task of undersea warfare with the detachment of the technician blended with an almost mystical sense of purpose. Perhaps it is this which gives them an errant mystery even to their brother officers in the Royal Navy.

But there are certain qualities which all possess – courage, youth, affection for and belief in the branch of the Navy which they serve. Consider the responsibility of a submarine captain, his task of handling and fighting what must be for her size the most complicated and deadly instrument of war. He must make his estimations and decisions rapidly and correctly. A slight error, an incorrect estimation, or a second's delay, because not only the failure of the attack but the destruction of the boat and her company.

Above all he must have the confidence of his men. Literally they look to him, for he alone knows what is happening in the sea and sky above. He stands crouched at the periscope, with a tacky film of oil and water under his feet and drops of seawater trickling from the periscope column onto his head. Watching silently and waiting for his next movement or order is the attack team – the first lieutenant, the plotting officer who operates the ingenious calculator called the "fruit machine," the torpedo officer, the telegraphists and the men at the hydroplanes controlling the vessel's depth and buoyancy. Their eyes are on the captain, and from his calmness and presence they take confidence. Four weeks he may not have had an hour's sleep or allowed himself entirely to relax; but he must betray no sign of fatigue, either an attack or counter-attack.

Submarine captains are young – "too old at 35" is a rule to which few exceptions are made – and the junior officers are correspondingly younger. Each has his sphere of duty and responsibility at sea and in harbour, but competence in that alone is not enough, for at any moment an officer may be called upon to perform another's duties.

After the Captain comes his second-in-command, the First Lieutenant. The organization of the ship's company, its division into watches, the allocation of duties to each man at diving and surfacing stations or when entering or leaving harbour – all this is the business of the first lieutenant. He supervises the cleanliness of the submarine, the maintenance of discipline, the employment and general welfare of the men, under continual practices and exercises necessary for fighting efficiency.

Another of his responsibilities is the care and maintenance of the storage batteries which drive the submarine when submerged. They are large and very heavy, accounting, in most submarines, for almost one-fifth of the total displacement; they are delicate and require much attention. But his most important duty is the maintenance of the vessel's trim – that is, her balance of stability when diving or surfacing. This demands a perfect understanding of the maze of pipes, valves, switches and handwheels, and of the ballast tanks with their vents and inlets, which regulate the trim.

Modern submarines have a thick hull inside a thin one. The pressure hull, as the thick one is called, is strong enough to resist the pressure of the sea at the maximum depth to which the submarine is designed to dive. (Sea pressure at 100 feet is approximately 45 lbs. per square inch.) The outside hull is the thin outer plating of the main ballast tanks and is not required to withstand sea pressure. When the submarine is submerged, the main ballast tanks are full and open to the sea, the pressure inside being automatically the same as that of the surrounding water.

When the submarine is on the surface, the main ballast tanks are open to the sea at the bottom; they are prevented from filling by air which is trapped and held inside by vent valves at the top. To make the submarine dive, the quick-acting vents are opened. The air is forced out of the tanks; the sea rushes in; the positive buoyancy of the vessel is destroyed and the submarine sinks. The angle at which she dives is determined by the hydroplanes, which are horizontal rudders, fitted forward and aft, that can be inclined to raise or lower the bow or stern.

The first lieutenant must see that the submarine remains steady at her depth, lying horizontal. Bad trim may cause her to break surface and disclose her position. A submarine is like a bicycle; balance is more easily maintained when she moves fast; one she stops, control is lost and she tends to topple over. But ability to move at very slow speed is essential for a submarine, particularly when she has reached her patrol area: then she seldom proceeds submerged at more than 2 knots, in order to conserve the battery power in case she is forced to stay down unusually long, or has to close for an attack at high-speed. If she is being hunted, she may have to lie stopped and silent, holding a "stopped trim," for the enemy can detect by asdic the turn of a motor or pump or even water gurgling into a tank. A submarine can only remain motionless if her trim is perfect.

When the submarine is perfectly balanced she said to be "in trim," being neither bodily heavy and trying to sink deeper nor bodily light and trying to rise. The depth of the submarine is maintained by the forward hydroplanes, and the angle by which she lies by the after ones. In order to be in trim, it is necessary to adjust the way to the submarine until it equals that of the seawater outside. This can be done by regulating the amount of water in the internal tanks which lie along the bottom of the pressure hull. Because they contain varying amounts of water and the pressure inside them is less than that of the sea outside, These tanks are fitted inside the pressure hole so that they will not be squashed in. They are called "internals."

The calculation's necessary to maintain trim must be continually checked and revised, for the consumption of fuel, fresh water, lubricating oil and food lightens the vessel, and so does the firing of torpedoes and guns.

Another man of many responsibilities is the engineer officer – a lieutenant (E), a warrant engineer, or, in small submarines, a chief engine room artificer.

The motive power of a submarine is provided from two sources, diesel oil engines and electric motors. A diesel engine requires air (which when mixed with oil forms a combustible fuel) and can therefore only be used when the vessel is on the surface. The diesel engines have two functions – propulsion, and the generation of electricity to charge the main storage batteries. Once submerged the diesel is valueless and power is provided by the electric motors which run off the batteries. These batteries are large and heavy and cannot be carried in great quantity; if big demands are made on them their energy is soon exhausted.

The efficiency of the machinery, complicated, delicate and compactly pressed into every available corner, is the responsibility of the engineer officer and those who work under him. When something goes wrong, knowledge, experience and a genius for improvisation must compensate for the limited supply of spare parts and tools which the vessel carries.

The submarine's main offensive weapon is the torpedo, a long cylinder 22 feet in length and 21 inches in diameter. It is propelled by an internal combustion engine burning a fuel which is a mixture of oil and air; it is kept at its depth by a hydrostatic valve and on course by gyroscope. At the forward end is a charge of high explosive and the apparatus for firing it when the torpedo strikes the target. It costs £2,500 and is as complicated a piece of mechanism for its size as the submarine itself. It is discharged by compressed air, its own engine being started in the process, and continues to run until it hits the target or runs out of fuel and sinks. Because the torpedo tubes are built into the hull structure, it is necessary to swing the submarine to aim the torpedo and release it on its correct course. Besides the torpedoes housed in the tubes, of which there are from four to eleven according to the class submarine, there are also spares. These are loaded by closing the outer end of the tube, emptying it of water and opening the inner end. The difficulty of handling a one-and-a-half ton torpedo within the restricted space can be imagined.

The torpedoes and gun armament are the responsibility of the officer next in seniority to the first lieutenant. He is usually lieutenant and is called the Third Hand.

The sub-lieutenant, known as the Fourth Hand, the navigator. Submerged by day and at night patrolling an unlit hostile coast, he can take advantage of few aids to navigation. The boat may be carried miles by an unexpected current as she lies stopped or moving at slow speed. Days may pass without a break in the clouds or a sight of the horizon to make it possible to fix the position by observation of the sun or stars.

In goes a torpedo, sliding down a ramp through the fore hatch. On the casing, stores wait to be loaded.

The navigator has many other duties – the correction of hundreds of charts with the latest information about buoys, lights, mined areas, swept channels, dangerous wrecks; the winding and checking of chronometers; the care and correction of the compasses and other navigational instruments. During a torpedo attack he usually works the "fruit machine." With the captain's estimations of the target's course and speed the "fruit machine" calculates how far ahead of the target the torpedo must be aimed.

Other duties are the running of the signal department, the safe keeping and correction of the secret and confidential books, I'm dealing with the deluge of official correspondence that arrives when the submarine reaches harbour.

The senior rating in the ship is the coxswain and chief petty officer. He is the first-lieutenant's right-hand man in the maintenance of discipline, in organising the employment of the men, and in ordering, stowing and issuing stores and provisions. He distributes the daily food rations, the rum and the four ounces of boiled sweets to each man.

The business end of a submarine – the tubes from which her torpedoes are fired by compressed air. In the racks are spares.

On the surface, he takes the wheel when a difficult manoeuvre calls for extra skill in handling the vessel, such as entering or leaving harbour, manoeuvering alongside another vessel, or during a surface action, when orders to put the rudder this way or that come rapidly from the captain on the bridge above. Diving or surfacing, or at moments of crisis below, he takes over the delicate job of operating the after hydroplanes.

The senior rating of the engineering department is the chief engine room artificer. In charge of the torpedo department, and responsible to the torpedo officer for the behaviour of the "fish," is the torpedo gunner's mate. He supervises their embarkation, stowage and charging with fuel and air, and the endless upkeep and testing which a torpedo requires. In action his place is that the fore ends making the final preparations for despatching the torpedoes. The petty officer telegraphist is in charge of the wireless equipment.

The outside engine room artificer is a specially selected rating, who has the responsible task of carrying out the orders to dive and surface the boat – the

The engine room is crammed with machinery. These are the diesels that drive the submarine when she is on the surface. They also generate power to charge the main storage batteries from which the electric motors are run.

opening and closing of main vents, the flooding and blowing of main ballast tanks. He or his mate raises and lowers the periscope during an attack and gets to know the captain's methods so that not a second is lost. He is also charged with maintaining the machinery, other than the electrical gear, outside the engine room. This includes the storage of the high pressure air which is used for many purposes, the most important being the forcing of the water from the main ballast tanks when the boat surfaces.

The gyro compass, torpedo-firing instruments and other electrical machines are in the care of the electrical artificer: a petty officer, qualified as a leading torpedo operator and known as the P.O. (L.T.O.), has charge of the main motors which drive the vessel submerged, the main batteries, lighting

"That small dim world below the sea." The men are as closely packed into the small space available as the machines: but there is a companionship in danger in a submarine that makes up for the discomfort.

and other electrical equipment. The orders given by the First Lieutenant for keeping the submarine in trim are carried out by a stoker petty officer.

The gunlayer's importance has only been fully recognised since the war; in peacetime he had little to do, and often combined his gunnery duties with those of the ship's cook.

These are the officers and some of the men who man a submarine; those unmentioned share equally in the tasks and trials, the penalties of disaster and the triumphs of success. The hazards of their life recall the words of Nelson before Copenhagen: "It is warm work and this day may be the last to any of us at a moment. But mark you! I would not be elsewhere for thousands."

The *Submarine Information and Instruction Manual* was an American publication produced in 1942, specifically for training men in the operation of the S-class submarine. By the time the United States entered the war in December 1941, the S-class submarines were of considerable vintage, the last of the 51 vessels being built in 1925, although S-class submarines remained in commission until 1946. The specifications of the S-class varied a little depending on the sub-variant (there were four major types of design within the class), but a typical "Group IV" specimen had displacements of 903 tons surfaced and 1,230 tons submerged, an overall length of 266ft (81.1m), a speed of 14.5 knots (27km/h) surfaced or 11 knots (20 km/h) submerged, a range of 8,000 nautical miles (15,000km) at 10 knots (19km/h) surfaced, and a crew of between 38 and 45 men.

The excerpt below is useful for explaining some of the core knowledge expected of submariners, especially their understanding of the layout, characteristics and performance of the submarine in general. Amongst submarine crews, it was imperative that each man to some degree understood the work of the other crew members; the small size of submarine crews meant that there was little duplication of roles, hence if a crucial individual was injured or killed, others had to step into their duties.

Submarine Information and Instruction Manual (1942)

GENERAL

The mission of the Submarine School is to equip enlisted men required for submarine service with an adequate foundation of theoretical and practical knowledge of submarines.

In carrying out this mission the basic Submarine School endeavors to explain the principles of all submarines, that is the principle of submergence and the control of the boat while submerged, and in addition the operation of and the details of construction of the hull and all the main internal fittings of an S-class submarine. By operation is meant the manning of the diving stations and the actual handling of the lines, valves, controls, tanks, etc. The S-class submarine has been picked as a type because its construction is comparatively simple. It should be borne in mind that basic principles will not vary between types of boats and that a thorough knowledge of an S-boat will enable a man to readily learn any of the later class submarines.

The instruction will proceed along the following lines:

Lectures:

1st Week.
> General Characteristics.
> Head Operation, Anchor Gear.

2nd Week.
> Buoyancy, Submarine Phraseology.
> Hull and Compartment Tests.

3rd Week.
> Trim Line and Pumps.
> Drainage System.
> Emergency Drills.

4th Week.
> Main Induction Line.
> Battery Ventilation System.
> Duties of Anchor Watch.
> Battery.

5th Week.
> High Pressure Air System.
> 100 lb. and Salvage Air System.

6th Week.
> Fuel Oil Compensating System and Lube Oil System.
> General Review, (all subjects).
> Mines.
> Deck Gun.
> CO_2, CO_2 Testing Outfit.
> Torpedoes.
> Bridge Routine, Visual Signals, Duties of Helmsman and Lookout.

Practical Work:

Operations in submarines at sea.
Instruction periods on submarines alongside dock.
Control submerged.

Instruction in submarine gun, and the use and safety precautions in handling a service automatic pistol.

Drill with arms.

Instruction in use of the submarine lung.

Note Book Work:

This work shall be as directed in these instructions. Note book work is essential to instruction because the knowledge obtained by sketching and digging out facts will be more readily retained by the student. All students are cautioned that the copying of notebooks of previous students defeats the purpose of the notebook and is strictly prohibited. Note books are the property of the student and should be retained by him and taken to sea. Note books will be taken to each instruction period held on board a submarine. Sketches should be referred to and various valves and machinery located and lines traced on the boat in conjunction with the sketch.

Note book work for each week will be completed by Friday noon and note books turned in to instructors at that time. Instructors will correct books and return them to student by Saturday noon.

Study:

The pamphlet issued each student is the text book for the course. All time not devoted to practical work is used for study and sketching.

All Hands Are Informed:

That the submarine service expects every man aboard from the captain on down to know his boat from the top mast to the keel. Knowledge of the entire boat is demanded, not just that required within a particular department or line of work.

That the hazardous nature of submarine operation demands from all detailed knowledge of construction, minute care in operation, and the highest attainable standard of attention to duty.

That though at sea the standard as regards uniform will necessarily follow the character of operations the high standard demanded in the U.S. Navy must be maintained in port and ashore. Each man is expected to maintain that high standard of his own accord.

That each man reporting aboard a submarine for duty is given six months in which to prepare himself to "Qualify for submarine duty." During that period he is expected to learn his particular boat as required in first paragraph.

That each man on a submarine will be given responsibility far exceeding that on any other type of naval vessel.

Now is the time for you to start preparation to fulfill the points listed in preceding paragraphs. The above has been told you at the beginning of your course. Guide yourself accordingly,

DEFINITIONS

The following definitions are promulgated for the information and guidance of the students at the Submarine School.

GENERAL

Submarine:
A vessel so constructed as to permit operation on the surface as a surface ship, and also having the ability to submerge and operate in a partially, or completely submerged condition.

Surface Condition Normal:
The submarine is in diving trim, with the main ballast and safety tanks empty.

Surface Condition, Emergency:
Main ballast tanks which are fitted as reserve fuel oil tanks actually full of oil, or oil and water. Other main ballast and safety tanks empty.

Submerged Condition:
Submarine operating with the "A" frames or highest part of structure under water.

Quick Dive:
A dive made from surface conditions when under way on one or more engines at the instant of sounding of the diving alarm.

Running Dive:
A dive made from surface conditions when under way on one or more motors at the instant of the diving alarm.

Stationary Dive:
A dive made when the boat is stopped and has no way on. The boat is trimmed down slowly by gradual addition of ballast water.

Riding the Vents:
A condition when the kingstons [for definition, see below] of a main ballast tank or safety tank are opened with the main vents closed.

Double Banking the Vents:
Consists of the following operation:
> Open the kingstons.
> Close the kingstons.
> Open the main vents.
> Close the main vents.
> Open the kingstons.

Rig For Diving:
A term embracing all the preparations, tests, and adjustments made inside and outside the boat prior to a dive.

Trim:
A condition of loading.

Diving Trim:
A trim in which the submarine is so compensated for weights that it can be quickly and safely submerged by the use of main ballast tanks, bow and stern planes and power plant.

Final Trim:
A trim at a particular depth where the submarine may be held at constant depth with minimum speed or at a speed designated and with limited use of planes.

Ventilate Inboard:
A condition of battery ventilation whereby the exhaust battery gases pass into the battery compartment.

Ventilate Outboard:
Same except gases pass outside pressure hull.

Venting a Tank:
The process of permitting air to pass into a tank (venting in) or to pass out of a tank (venting out) as water or other liquid leaves or enters the tank.

Blowing a Tank:
The process of admitting compressed air into the top of a tank containing water or other liquid with the flood valves at the bottom open.

STRUCTURAL

Main Ballast Tanks:
Tanks provided primarily to furnish buoyancy on the surface, and which are habitually carried full of water when submerged, excepting tanks whose main volume is above the surface water line. It is the flooding of these tanks which destroys positive buoyancy.

Safety Tanks:
Main ballast tanks designed for quick blowing or pumping.

Buoyancy Tanks:
Ballast tanks with their main volume above the water line, designed for quick blowing in emergency. They are free flooding, vent controlled, and may be either "bow" or "stern" buoyancy tanks.

Variable Tanks:
Ballast tanks not habitually carried full of water when submerged, and designed for weight compensation. Forward trim tank, after trim tank and auxiliary come under this heading.

Trimming Tanks:
The variable tanks nearest the bow and stern of the boat. Known as forward trim and after trim tanks respectively.

W. R. T. Tanks (Water Round Torpedo):
Variable tanks located near torpedo tubes and designed to carry enough water to fill up the space between the torpedo and the tubes.

Regulating Tanks:
Small variable tanks designed for water measuring and constructed to stand greater pressure than other ballast tanks.

Auxiliary Tanks:
Variable ballast tanks located at or near the center of gravity of the boat, and designed for weight compensation.

Main Compartments:
All main compartments are designated as rooms with a prefix denoting their principal use as: torpedo room, engine room, etc.

Diving Planes:
Rudders used for controlling the vertical motion of the vessel when submerged. Forward set are designed "bow planes" and after set as "stern planes."

Outer Hull:
The portion of the vessel forming the external boundary of it, regardless of weight, type or tightness of plating.

Inner Hull:
That portion of the double hull submarine forming longitudinal boundary of the main compartments regardless of weight type or tightness of plating.

Pressure Hull:
That portion of a submarine, which, under normal submerged operation, may be at any, or all times subject to full pressure of submergence.

Main Vents and Stops:
Large valves used to permit the air in main ballast tanks to be forced outside the pressure hull as the flooding water enters the tanks.

Kingstons:
Large valves of sliding type which are located at the bottom of the main ballast tanks to allow passage of water into or out of the tanks.

BUOYANCY

Archimedes Principle:
A body immersed in a liquid is buoyed up by a force equal to the weight of the liquid displaced by it.

Positive Buoyancy:
The condition of a body immersed in a liquid, in which the body is capable of displacing a weight of the liquid greater than its own weight. Hence it floats.

Negative Buoyancy:
The condition of a body immersed in a liquid in which the body is incapable of displacing a weight of the liquid equal to or greater than its own weight. Hence it sinks.

Neutral Buoyancy:
The condition of a body immersed in a liquid in which the body displaces a weight of the liquid exactly equal to its own weight. Hence the body has no tendency to either sink or come to the surface of the liquid.

Neutral Point:
The point in the ballasting of a submarine at which neutral buoyancy occurs.

Reserve Buoyancy:
The difference between the weight of surface displacement of a submarine in diving trim, and her displacement when submerged in neutral buoyancy with all main ballast tanks completely filled. In other words the amount of ballast that must be taken on board to change her from the surface condition to the submerged condition in neutral buoyancy.

The Fleet Type Submarine, Navpers 16160, was a US Navy submariner training manual produced in 1946, shortly after the end of World War II. Although it post-dates the conflict, the manual remains useful to our study here, as it essentially collected and presented much of the expertise that had just been gathered in wartime conditions. The following passage explains some of the key training devices used aboard US submarines, specifically those relating to making attacks, diving and operating the torpedo tubes. Regarding the latter, during World War II submarines tended to have 4–8 torpedo tubes, typically mounted in the bows, but some types also had stern tubes for rearward firing. The torpedoes were pushed out of the flooded tubes via compressed air, at which point their own internal motors would take over, carrying the torpedo, depending on the type, to ranges between a few hundred yards to several miles. All the routines described here were critical to the submarine's survival, hence had to be practised until they could be performed with near unconscious speed.

The Fleet Type Submarine, Navpers 16160 (1946)

SUBMARINE TRAINING DEVICES
A. GENERAL

21A1. Introductory. The modern feet-type submarine is an exceedingly complex mechanism. On the surface, in normal operation, it presents all the problems of ship handling and navigation common to surface vessels. Its problems do not end there, however, for when it submerges it becomes, in effect, an entirely different vessel with new characteristics and new problems.

Submerged, the control becomes more complicated; the ship must be navigated in a three-dimensional medium and many conditions affecting its operation are much more critical than when it is on the surface. Added to these complexities are the more limited facilities for observation and the necessity of relying, to a great extent, on dead reckoning.

As the submarine is an offensive weapon, its chief value against the enemy is its ability to approach undetected and to maneuver to a firing position despite the target's efforts to avoid contact. The approach and attack phase of submarine warfare is a science in itself, requiring a practiced eye, an analytical mind, and the ability to make swift and accurate decisions. Though the possession of these attributes is a paramount requirement for submarine officers, to be of value in submarine attack they must be supplemented with long experience and thorough training.

In the early days of the submarine this experience and training were acquired through actual service under a competent commanding officer. With the growth of the fleet and the phenomenal development of the submarine and its equipment, it became evident that qualified personnel must be secured in ever increasing numbers and trained more rapidly. To this end, numerous training devices, duplicating the more important features of a submarine, have been developed and may be used to simulate actual situations encountered or patrols.

Three departments of the submarine have been the object of particular attention, the conning tower, the control room, and the torpedo room, resulting in the production of three devices known as the *attack teacher*, the *diving trainer* and the *torpedo tube trainer*. These devices are used to train fire-control parties, diving officers, and control room personnel, and to instruct in the care and manipulation of torpedoes and torpedo tubes and in the firing of torpedoes.

B. THE ATTACK TEACHER

21B1. Description. The attack teacher is a device by which typical approach and attack problems may be duplicated in all their phases. The fire-control party in training is assembled in a mock-up conning tower. Miniature models of enemy vessels are maneuvered in the field of a specially designed periscope and the fire-control party simulates the conduct of an actual operation against an enemy.

Early attack teachers bore little resemblance to the devices of the present day. Like the submarines, they have developed rapidly, and they now afford a reliable presentation of battle problems and facilities for their solutions.

C. THE DIVING TRAINER

21C1. Description. The diving trainer (see figure) consists of a duplicate of the port side of the control room with all the apparatus and equipment usually installed in that section of the submarine. The control room section is mounted so that it may be tilted to assume all the normal up-and-down angles encountered in the actual operation of a submarine. The instruments and controls are mounted in their relative locations and all function just as when actually installed on a submarine.

The device is operated from a control stand in front of the room. This stand is the station of the instructor and affords him a full view of all the gages, instruments, and members of the control room personnel. The controls not normally installed on the port side of the control room are mounted in their relative positions at the side of the lecture room.

The diving trainer.

Electric and hydraulic controls enable the instructor to create conditions which are normally encountered and registered on the instruments. The student, acting as diving officer, then issues the necessary orders to attain the desired condition of the submarine. Every action necessary to diving, trimming, and surfacing the ship is carried out to the most exact detail and the response of the tilting section of the control room and the registry of the gages indicate to the student the same result as would be obtained with an actual submarine.

The use of this trainer has shortened the training period otherwise necessary and permits the training of an increased number of students.

D. THE TORPEDO TUBE TRAINER

21D1. Description. A recent innovation in training devices is an installation of a standard torpedo tube with all controls, interlocks, and mechanisms, and from which a standard torpedo may be fired and the procedure observed. (See figure)

The torpedo tube trainer.

The tube itself is an exact duplicate of those installed in the fleet-type submarines. The tube is mounted on the end of a water tight tank in which varying pressures, corresponding to assumed depths, can be attained. The torpedo tube muzzle extends into the tank and is fitted with the standard muzzle door. Guides along the bottom of this tank, and above the course of the fired torpedo, are installed to prevent any erratic course once the torpedo leaves the tube.

Heavy glass windows in the side of the tank permit observations to be made of the torpedo's exit from the tube and the amount of bubble checked.

The torpedo is loaded into the tube and is fired in a normal manner and at normal speeds. At the rear end of the tank the torpedo enters a restricted passage. The water expelled from this passage exhausts through gradually reduced orifices and the torpedo is brought to a gentle stop. It is then pushed back through the tank and tube to the loading rack where it may be used again.

A gyro angle indicator regulator is mounted near the tube and any normal operation connected with torpedo fire may be duplicated.

CHAPTER 2
MAINTENANCE, DRILLS AND ROUTINES

E fficiency was the critical factor in submarine operations. Every action had to be streamlined and perfected, so it could be implemented in action quickly and decisively. In the first passage below, from the 1942 publication *Submarine Information and Instruction Manual*, we not only see descriptions of some of the basic routine procedures aboard a US submarine, but also an extensive list of "General Safety Instructions and Operating Notes". From this list, it is evident that training and experience had to impart a huge spectrum of knowledge to the submariners, everything from the right way to close and secure hatches through to the dangers of obscuring vents with clothing. The manual also explains what to do in a variety of emergencies, including that of abandoning ship underwater. In this context, the reference to the "lungs" is actually to the Momsen Lung rebreather device, a system for providing temporary respiration while escaping to the surface from a submerged submarine. Using such devices was unpredictable and dangerous. There is only actually one instance of Momsen Lung use in the war, when 13 men of the USS *Tang* escaped from a forward compartment on 24 October 1944, after the submarine was hit in action by its own torpedo, which malfunctioned and took a circular path. Only five of the escapees, however, survived at the surface.

Submarine Information and Instruction Manual (1942)

STEPS FOR GETTING TORPEDO TUBE
READY FOR FIRING

In the control room, throw in torpedo firing circuit switch, located on switchboard, or radio room bulkhead.

See air on 100 lb. line forward.

See high pressure air line to torpedo room is open.

Open forward trim line blow valve on air manifold. In torpedo room (1) flood the torpedo tubes from forward trim Lank, (2) open the shutters to desired tubes, (3) open the tube outer doors, (4) see curve firing gear disengaged, (5) check ready lights, (6) open stop valve from air line to solenoids, volume tank, open independent valve to solenoid H. P. (there is one valve for each solenoid,) (7) build up pressure from H.P. line to impulse tank to 135 lbs., (8) crack and open the firing valve stop, (9) throw in tube ready light switch.

The torpedo is now ready to be fired, electrically, from the control room. When the firing key is pressed, the solenoid is energized and lifts

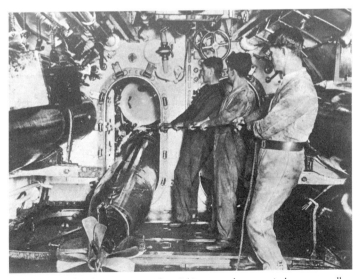

Aboard a British submarine, a torpedo weighing more than a ton is drawn manually into a torpedo tube.

the solenoid off its seat, allowing the air from solenoid to enter the stop bolt cylinder behind the piston, forcing the stop bolt rod forward and withdrawing the stop bolt from in front of the torpedo drive stud. As the piston moves forward, it uncovers a port, allowing the air to continue to the after end of the over balanced piston; when the air enters the after side of the over balanced piston it overcomes the overbalanced condition of the firing valve, allowing the firing valve to open. The impulse air then enters the tube, forcing the torpedo from the tube. The tripping latch strikes the starting lever as the torpedo moves forward, and starts the torpedo under its own power.

COMMON NOTES OF IMPORTANCE FOR GENERAL KNOWLEDGE

Normal air (the air we breathe) is simple mixtures (not a chemical combination) of the following gases:

Nitrogen (approx.)	78% by volume
Oxygen	21% by volume
Hydrogen and certain inert gases & traces of Carbon Dioxide (approx.)	1% by volume

Nitrogen is non-inflammable, colorless, tasteless and odorless.

Hydrogen in its pure state is a colorless, tasteless, odorless gas. It is the lightest substance known. It is very inflammable.

These two (Nitrogen and Hydrogen) gases as occurring in the atmosphere have no affect on the human body other than to dilute the oxygen as well as CO_2 and likewise any poisonous gases which may be present.

HOW TO FIRE A SIGNAL GUN

See that signal gun is drained by opening secure drain valve, secure drain valve.

Open breech door with operating lever by the left.

See that holding button in barrel of gun is working freely.

Load rocket half way into gun, pull out safety pin, shove rocket home.

Close breech door by swinging operating lever to the right, press in on button on operating lever, continuing to swing lever to the right, opening the muzzle door.

Open supply valve from 100 lb. air line to firing lever. Hold firing lever open 10 seconds. Secure gun when fired.

HOW TO OPERATE THE HEAD

Open sea valve and stop, flood water into upper chamber as desired. Secure sea valve and stop.

Operate counter weight lever and allow water to pass into lower chamber (after releasing lever, make sure gasket seats properly).

Open stop on 100 lb. air supply.

By use of rocker valve, charge volume tank to 15 lbs. over sea pressure.

Open sea valve on discharge line from lower bowl, open quick opening valve from lower bowl.

Push rocker valve over to "Blow" (holding about 5 seconds.) Release rocker valve.

Secure quick opening valve, secure sea valve.

Vent remainder of pressure in volume tank into bilges (by putting rocker valve to "Vent") .

[. . .]

GENERAL SAFETY INSTRUCTION AND OPERATING NOTES

Never attempt to blow a partially filled tank to sea while submerged.

Reason:

Water will flow into the tank before air pressure will be built up in excess of that outside, with result that negative buoyancy will be obtained. Exception – Blowing of small regulator tank of 0, R and S class permissible regardless of amount of water in tank.

While operating either surfaced or submerged, have all water tight doors free for quick closing.

Reason:

In event of collision, any obstruction to the doors may prevent rapid closing of doors with resultant spread of water.

While the engines are operating, never close any doors between the control room and engine room.

Reason:

To do so will permit the engines to be supplied with air only by the main induction. This line is normally not large enough to supply sufficient air with result engines will pull a vacuum in the boat. The vacuum and the rush of air when it is filled will produce physical hardship such as nose bleed, ruptured ear drums, etc.

While the engines are operating never close the main induction.

Reason:

If with main induction closed, a door between the control room and engine room were closed, the engines would have no air supply and would pull such a vacuum in the engine room that it would probably be fatal to all personnel present.

Never ventilate the battery outboard in any weather rough enough to put spray on the deck.

Reason:

Even a small amount of salt water mixing with the battery acid will cause a large amount of chlorine gas to be given off. The gas is not only deadly to personnel, but injurious to the battery. Ridding the battery of the chlorine compounds formed in the plates is a slow process during which the boat must be laid up.

If during a battery charge a blower should stop, no attempt should be made to start it. Always secure the charge and keep remaining blower running.

Reason:

A battery being charged gives off a gas called hydrogen, the greatest amount being given off when the battery is gassing heavily toward the end of the charge. Hydrogen is a highly explosive gas which will rapidly accumulate in the battery ducts should the blowers stop. On restarting blower, a spark may be caused by the reforming of the moisture films within the ducts which igniting the hydrogen would cause an explosion disastrous to both personnel and material. Therefore, if blower has stopped or is running improperly, stop charge and make no attempt to restart blower until one hour after gassing has stopped.

During a battery charge, especially while gassing, permit no smoking or any naked lights in battery compartment or in vicinity of battery exhaust.

Reason:

Danger of hydrogen explosion.

After a battery compartment has been sealed for any appreciable time due to fire or any other reason, remember that hydrogen will be present in the compartment. The amount will depend upon the working of the battery prior to or during sealing of the compartment. In any case, after unsealing, permit no naked lights either in or in vicinity of the compartment. Do not start battery blowers or any other machinery in the compartment. Allow battery to ventilate naturally. After four hours, provided tests indicate low hydrogen content, danger may be considered to be over.

On rig for diving, see by visual examination that all hull openings except main induction are securely closed. Don't place all your faith on indicators.

Reason:
To be certain beyond all doubt that the openings are closed.

Never enter tanks which are normally closed, such as fuel tank and main and variable ballast tanks, until they have been thoroughly aired out. Then, all men working inside must be watched by men outside tank. Also, attach line to men going into large tanks.

Reason:
Such tanks may contain air lacking in oxygen or harmful gasses which may produce unconsciousness and death. Fuel tanks may in addition contain explosive gasses.

Before starting machinery see that it is clear for operating.

Reason:
Obstructions in the way of gears, shafting, etc., will cause serious damage if not removed prior to turning machinery. This applies to the main machinery as well as the various auxiliaries.

All diving stations must be kept manned until they have been secured on order "secure from dive".

Reason:
To be ready to dive again.

Never flood torpedo tubes from sea without first seeing all tube drain valves and forward trim flood valve secured.

Reason:
Water flooded into tubes and passing into forward trim will produce negative buoyancy.

When underway, always keep all gear in superstructure, especially mooring lines, secured in such a manner that it cannot get out of the lockers.

Reason:

A line wrapped around a propeller will disable that shaft. Other gear striking the propeller will do it more or less damage causing vibration.

While submerged, never set up on the dogs of the deck hatches.

Reason:

The pressure of the sea during the dive will make the hatch dogs appear to be loose because the hatch has been forced down. If tightened in this condition, the hatch upon surfacing may be so tight that it cannot be opened.

Avoid touching electric cables or antenna wires while hands or decks are wet.

Reason:

Dampness increases the possibility of grounding the current through the body.

Never use water from battery tank for drinking or cooking purposes.

Reason:

Tank is lead lined and may cause lead poisoning.

Never permit smoking or naked lights while handling ammunition on or taking on fuel oil.

Reason:

Fumes given off may be readily ignited, resulting in an explosion or bad fire.

Never drill, strike or deform any flasks or piping carrying compressed air or any other gas.

Reason:

A rupture would result in explosion with attendant danger to personnel and material.

Never allow charged air flasks, such as torpedo air flasks or oxygen bottles, to be exposed to the direct rays of the sun or to any heat.

Reason:

Pressure within flasks will be increased by heat and may be raised sufficiently to cause rupture.

Never allow ammunition of any kind to be exposed to the direct rays of the sun or to any heat.

Reason:
Causes deterioration of powder which may produce instability or improper ballistic qualities.

After surfacing, hull openings, except (1) the conning tower hatch and (2) the main induction, shall be left closed until the boat has finally been rigged for surface.

Reason:
Boat cannot be considered in an entirely stable condition until main ballast tanks have been pumped dry and vents, kingstons, drains and pumps are secured.

Never open the inner door of a torpedo tube until check has been made to see (1) that tube is dry and (2) that outer door is closed.

Reason:
To prevent outer and inner door being opened at the same time, which if it happened, would result in the loss of the boat. Mechanical interlocks are provided to prevent this from happening, but check just the same.
    Before opening up any tank, vent to relieve any pressure and inspect to see all valves through which water could possibly enter tank are securely closed.

When order to surface is given all main ballast tank vents should be closed whether or not specifically ordered closed.

Reason:
To prevent air used for blowing from passing overboard without blowing water from tank.

When using a fire extinguisher in an enclosed space, wear a gas mask which protects against CO_2.

Reason:
Fire extinguishers have as their principle the smothering of the fire by excluding the air. It will do the same to humans, producing suffocation.

The use of water to extinguish fires in a submarine should be avoided.

Reason:
To avoid electrical shocks; to avoid spread of oil; to prevent formation of chlorine.

Never hang clothing on battery ventilation suction or discharge lines.

Reason:

Flow of air through battery will be restricted, causing increase of hydrogen present with danger of explosion.

Small drains of main and battery induction lines shall habitually be kept open. Drains should be frequently tested to see that they are clear.

Reason:

So that if leaks occur in the line, their presence will be known immediately. Drains will frequently become plugged by the lead sulphate formed by the action of the acid gas on the lead lining of the battery induction piping. This lead sulphate lying in the pipes will eventually work its way into the drains and plug them up.

No one except necessary personnel shall be permitted on the bridge from the time "rig for diving" has been ordered until "rig for surface" has been ordered.

A submarine engine room, in which not an inch of space is wasted.

Reason:
Boat during this period must be ready to dive at a moment's notice.
[. . .]

WATCH STANDING

After joining your submarine one of the most important duties that you will be given will be the anchor watch. The anchor watch is a man in the duty section who is assigned a topside watch whenever the submarine is anchored or moored. The anchor watch is directly responsible to the Commanding Officer for the safety of the ship and crew. For this reason it is absolutely necessary that the anchor watch be a reliable man who knows his boat and his job. One thing should be thoroughly impressed on your mind when you have the anchor watch – if anything extraordinary happens or any emergency arises **DO NOT HESITATE** to call the duty officer, the duty chief and the duty section. Smart and quick action on the part of the anchor watch has prevented many a casualty in the submarine service. Whereas on a large ship the anchor watch is more or less a messenger, on a submarine the anchor watch is in reality officer of the deck. You must be able to assume the trust that is given you when you take over the anchor watch-otherwise you will never be a good submarine man and if you are not a **GOOD** submarine man you will not be retained in the submarine service. When you stand your first few anchor watches you will be under the critical eye of the duty officer, and the duty chief. Be **VIGILANT** then and continue to be vigilant every minute of every anchor watch that you ever stand.

The following instructions were taken from the ship's orders of an S-boat. They are used as a guide to students. Each particular submarine has its own orders and instructions to the anchor watch. Assure yourself that you know and understand the orders and instructions before taking over the watch.

The Specific Duties of the Anchor Watch are as Follows:

Enter in the Quartermaster's notebook all items required for entry in the log. This shall be at times indicated by the quartermaster.

Report movements of ships and unusual occurrences to the duty chief and duty officer.

Keep informed of the ships present and the Senior Officer present afloat.

Meet and salute at the gangway all officers boarding or leaving the ship. The anchor watch shall attend such officers until told to carry on or his duties require him elsewhere.

Keep a sharp lookout for signals and approaching boats. Inform the duty officer and commanding officer when any senior officer approaches the gangway.

Receive and take charge of packages coming on board, turning them over to the addressee or the commanding officer.

Keep informed as to the whereabouts of the duty section, duty chief, duty officer, and the ship's officers. Report to the next senior officer when the commanding officer leaves the ship.

Visitors will not be allowed on board without the permission of the duty officer.

Keep men topside in the uniform of the day except at night and during working hours.

See that ship's routine and any special orders are carried out.

See that colors are made and anchor lights turned on and off promptly.

Sound attention for passing ships, barges or gigs passing close aboard with flag or colors flying.

Report to duty officer the arrival of all stores and provisions.

Return all salutes to the colors by officers and men corning on deck or leaving the ship.

Report any fire hazards immediately to the duty chief and investigate thoroughly any condition that seems unusual.

BELOW DECK WATCH

In All Compartments:
Listen for the sound of dripping water or escaping air.

Note any unusual odor.

Note any smell of smoke.

See that electric heaters are clear of clothing and bunks.

Note anything unusual in the compartment.

See that ship's ventilation system is operating properly.

Torpedo Room:
All sea and stop valves secured.

Bilges are dry.

Note reading on forward trim tank gauge.

Note pressure readings on torpedo tube gauges, (should never exceed five (5) pounds).

Trim line valves closed.

Note pressure on forward fuel group, (should be 0).

Forward Battery:

Inspect by placing hand over the two intakes that there is a suction of air into the battery ventilation system.

Determine that the battery ventilation blowers are running as prescribed by Engineer Officer.

Inspect to see that dampers and lower and upper flapper valves on the battery ventilation are secured in the open position.

Inspect to see that the 1 and 2 main ballast tank vent and stop valves are closed.

Control Room:

Note the pressure readings on all main and variable ballast tank gauges – this pressure should never exceed 5 lbs.

Note the reading in degrees of the inclinometer (athwart-ships trim) and the degrees on the fore and aft trim indicator.

Note the pressure readings on all air bank gauges. See that at least one air bank having a minimum of 1500 lbs. pressure is connected up to the manifold.

Note and clearly determine that the control room bilges and periscope wells are dry.

See that all sea and stop valves are closed, including the conning tower flood valve.

See that valves on trim manifold are secured. See that kingstons are closed and locked.

After Battery:

Inspect by placing hand over the two intakes that there is a suction of air into the battery ventilation system.

Determine that the battery ventilation blowers are running as prescribed by Engineer Officer.

Inspect and see that the dampers and the lower and upper flapper valves on the battery ventilation system are secured in the open position.

Inspect and see that outboard battery ventilation flapper valve is secured open.

Inspect to see that the after main ballast tank vent and stop valves are closed.

See that all sea and stop valves are closed.

Note that ice machine is running properly.

Engine Room:

Note and clearly determine the height of water in the engine room bilges. If over a safe height report same to duty chief immediately.

See that sea valves on head are closed and not leaking. See that all sea and stop valves are closed.

Motor Room:
Note and clearly determine the height of water in the motor room bilges. If above a safe height report same to duty chief immediately.

See that all sea and stop valves are closed.

See that trim line valves are closed.

The Following Shall Be Checked Frequently About The Topside:
See that the battery ventilation exhausts in the fairwater are clear.

Reading of draft marks.

When moored – inspect the mooring lines; at anchor – inspect the anchor chain and drift lead.

See that topside is clean and neat with no loose gear, newspapers, etc., about.

The check-off list shall be kept in accordance with the form furnished. The items thereon shall be checked by actual inspection and not as a matter of form at the end of each watch.

The anchor watch will call his relief fifteen minutes before the end of his watch, and he will not be considered as properly relieved unless the watch is relieved on deck with both men in complete uniform.

Pressures in the main or variable ballast tanks, fuel groups, or torpedo tubes shall not be vented. Whenever the pressure in any one of these reaches 5 lbs. the duty chief shall be called and he will be responsible for taking appropriate action.

In case of doubt as to what to do, or in case of anything that appears unusual the anchor watch will call the duty chief at once and a thorough investigation shall be conducted. Do not hesitate to call the entire section if it appears that the conditions warrant it. In the case of electrical casualties, such as failure of battery ventilation, call the electrician's mate of the watch and the duty chief. In the event of any condition that cannot be handled easily and immediately by the anchor watch, the duty chief shall be called. Constant supervision by the entire section is necessary at all times.

DRILLS AND EXERCISES

The instructions for emergencies are issued for information and guidance. All hands must realize that the laying down of implicit instructions to cover each and every situation is impossible. Therefore all hands are reminded that the successful handling of emergencies must depend upon the cool logical action of men who know their submarine and who have ingrained in them the basic actions demanded of them by each emergency. The cardinal principle of all damage control is-as quickly as possible prevent the spread of damage. With that one principle in mind an intelligent man who knows his boat can do little wrong. Know then, what to do, when to do it, how to do it, and why you do it.

All persons discovering leaks, chlorine, fire, etc., shall immediately pass the word as to nature and location and then shall take every action to combat the situation. Passing the word is necessary to bring others to assist; quick action may prevent a dangerous situation from developing.

The emergencies which may be encountered in the normal operation of submarines are:

Collision – The greatest threat to the submarine is collision on the surface.

Fire – Oil or electrical fires are the most probable.

Chlorine – This is the evolution of a deadly gas produced when salt water is mixed with sulphuric acid.

Abandon Ship – May be either necessary with boat on surface or when boat on bottom by the use of the lung.

Man overboard.

Collision – Surface:

The boat must expect a large inflow of water which if not confined will be sufficient to rapidly produce negative buoyancy and take the boat under. In general, to prevent this, seal up the affected compartment and make the pressure hull tight as for diving:

Close doors to affected compartment. Close all deck hatches.

Close main induction and flappers.

Close battery overboard discharge valve and seal battery tanks.

Put gags in compartment salvage line in unaffected compartments.

Put three banks of air on the manifold. Keep 100 lbs. air built up. Stand by to turn on salvage air.

Put high pressure pump on trim line.

Stand by low pressure pump.

Stand by to put any tank or bilges on the trim line or main drain or to blow any tank including fuel oil tanks or tubes to sea.

Stop motor (if ordered) and put batteries and motors in highest power combination, i.e., batteries in series, motors in parallel.

Expect any orders to motors or engines. If collision is imminent maximum speed ahead may do more good than attempted backing. **CAUTION**: If continuing ahead on the engines, alter collision alarm standby W. T. doors and main induction but do not close.

Close all small openings between compartments, as battery compartment drains and voice tubes.

Collision – Submerged:

The decision as to whether or not to surface or go deeper must rest with the commanding officer.

In general provisions given above apply equally well submerged as on the surface for the main thing is to restrict flooding to affected compartment.

If Order "Surface" Is Given:

Blow all ballast tanks hard.

Close all W.T. doors.

Put H.P. pump on trim line.

Put L.P. pump on main drain.

Put batteries in series. Go ahead full speed on motors.

Hard rise bow and stern planes.

Stand by to put any tank or bilges on trim line or main drain or to blow any tanks including fuel oil tanks and tubes to sea.

Put gags in unaffected compartments.

Seal battery tanks by securing ventilation and closing flappers.

Close all small openings between compartments as battery compartment drains, voice tubes, galley ventilation.

Stand by for chlorine if collision is in a battery compartment.

If Order "Surface" Is Not Given:

Close all W.T. doors.

Put gags in unaffected compartments. Put H.P. pump on trim line.

Stand by to put any tank or bilges on the trim line or main drain or to blow any tanks including fuel tanks and torpedo tubes to sea.

Seal battery tanks by securing ventilation and closing flappers.

Close all small openings between compartments as battery compartment drains, voice tubes and galley ventilation.

All hands be ready to bring boat to surface.

Expect chlorine if collision is in battery compartment.

Orders regarding speed will come from Commanding Officer.

Fire:
If alongside dock or other vessel make preparations for getting underway.

If submerged, surface provided it can be done in safety.

Fight Fire and Attempt To Extinguish It By Cutting Down Air Supply Or By Physical Smothering As Follows:
Shut off ventilation system.

Turn off fans.

If in control room or aft of it stop main engines.

Remove detonaters from affected compartment.

Secure battery charge – **CAUTION:** Whether or not to secure the battery ventilation if charging batteries will depend upon officer in charge.

Securing the ventilation of a gassing battery may produce a situation of more danger than a fire.

Stand by to close doors to adjacent compartments.

Beat out fire by smothering with blankets or mattresses.

If above does not succeed use fire extinguisher.

CAUTION:
Fire extinguishers have as their principle the generation of a gas which acts to smother the fire by excluding the air. It naturally will also, in a confined space, exclude air from humans and produce suffocation. Therefore, when using extinguishers in a confined space as will always exist in a submarine, the persons applying the extinguisher should wear gas masks or leave the compartment.

CAUTION:
The use of water should be avoided because of the attendant danger of severe electrical shock. Never use water to extinguish an electric fire.

CAUTION:
Use only fire extinguisher which has carbon tetrachloride as its agency against electric fires. With other liquid types severe electric shocks may be suffered.

CAUTION:
Never use water on an oil fire.

If fire is in compartment where explosives are stored stand by to flood magazines on orders from officer in charge. Explosives not in magazines shall if possible be removed from the scene of the fire but if too large to be moved, protect by cooling water or tarpaulin.

If fire is in battery compartment take load off that battery.

If in spite of the above, the fire cannot be controlled, or in event of a rather serious fire submerged and boat cannot be surfaced, seal up the compartment with no one inside and fire will eventually be smothered.

Chlorine:

This is poisonous gas, a few breaths of which will produce serious injury to the lungs or death. It has very powerful odor and is pea green in color. These characteristics make it very easily detected. The gas is heavier than air and has a tendency to settle down into the bilges or the decks.

In Event of Chlorine Proceed as Follows:

When occurring on the surface:

Seal compartment.

Close watertight doors to affect compartment (stop engines as ordered by bridge; the W.T. doors of after battery cannot be closed until they are stopped).

Close battery compartment drains to torpedo, control, or engine room as appropriate.

Close main induction flapper (after battery).

Close galley vent in engine room in after battery.

Secure battery ventilation.

Take load off affected battery.

Secure battery charge.

Officer and electrician enter compartment wearing gas masks to determine cause of chlorine and having discovered it, attempt to remove the cause. Then open battery ventilation lines and ventilate outboard at full speed.

When Occurring While Submerged:

Seal the battery compartment.

Surface and proceed as above. In surfacing, never blow the tank under the affected battery because the existence of chlorine may be caused by a leak in the tank top of the main ballast and blowing will drive more water into the tank. Blow other tanks and close kings-ton of the tank under battery. Commence pumping tank as quickly as possible.

Stop motors and cut out affected battery, then use but one battery for propulsion. Passage of current through a sea water affected battery greatly increases the emission of chlorine.

In event it is not possible to surface, seal the compartment and cut out the affected battery. Surface and clear the boat as soon as circumstances permit.

Abandon Ship:

Surface:

All hands except watch proceed quickly up conning tower to deck.

After these men are clear, the watch pass life jackets up hatch. In order to render life jackets readily available, men should bring them from other compartments en route to control room and deposit them on deck of control room.

Watch secure ship as for collision if time permits, then follow up hatch.

Mattress, deck grating, etc., should if possible be thrown overboard to provide floating material to which men in the water may cling.

Submerged:

The following procedure is copied from "Doctrine to Govern Submarine Escape Operations". In an emergency necessitating the abandonment of a vessel the following steps should be taken in effecting escape:

Make all necessary preparations for flooding the compartment. Secure the bulkheads for watertightness. See that the hatch skirt is in position and secured. Un-dog the hatch and secure with a stout line to some solid fitting in the compartment. Open the valves in the oxygen line and set the reducer to exceed by 20 lbs. the depth pressure when the compartment is flooded.

Break out lungs. Remove from cloth bags. Remove cellophane from flutter valves. Put on lungs, adjusting neck strap so that the lung can be held comfortably in the mouth. Adjust strap around waist, leaving about two inches of slack. Secure trouser clips well taut.

Flood the compartment. Open every available sea connection. Remove bonnets from valves backing up sea valves and open sea valves. In the motor room the bonnet on the L.P. ballast pump suction valve should be removed and the discharge valve opened. The outer doors of torpedo tubes may be opened and the compartment flooded through the inboard vents and through the drains after the valve bonnets are removed.

Wrenches suitable for all nuts which must be removed should be stowed in each compartment; also a maul and pinch bar. Flooding once begun should be done as quickly as possible as danger from exposure to pressure depends upon the time for exposure. As flooding proceeds men must clear their ears by swallowing, or working their jaws as in chewing, or by holding the nose and blowing, thereby putting a pressure on the inner side of the ear drums. Inability to clear the ears will be painful but will not result in permanent injury. When the pressure inside the boat equals the outside water pressure, flooding will automatically stop. The line holding the hatch should then be

The "Momsen Lung" emergency escape breathing device is used by a US submariner during submarine's sea trials in July 1930.

cut. The hatch spring and a slightly greater pressure on the lower side of the hatch should cause the hatch to open completely. A heavy stream of water will enter until the trunk is flooded and the water level in the compartment reaches the bottom of the hatch skirt. In depths such that the pressure is not equalized by the time the water reaches the bottom of the hatch skirt, compressed air, if available, should be admitted into compartment. If the hatch is not completely opened, a man equipped with a charged lung can go up the ladder and push the hatch open. This man then re-enters the compartment.

When the hatch is open, stream the buoy; when it watches, secure the line to a rung of the ladder or other secure object.

With the shut-off valve in mouthpiece closed, and with flutter valve submerged, charge lung with oxygen.

Put mouthpiece in mouth, exhale completely through the nose, put on the noseclip, open mouthpiece valve and commence breathing.

Breathe oxygen for about two minutes before beginning the ascent. This can be accomplished by having men who are standing by charge their own lungs from spare oxygen containers. No delay in making ascents should be caused by waiting for this two-minute interval. During this time see that there is no marked resistance to breathing, either inhaling or exhaling. If soda lime dust is drawn into the mouth and throat it should be spat out before the man enters the water.

The mouthpiece should be gripped properly; the teeth clamped down, not too tightly on the rubber lugs; the rubber flange between the lips and the teeth, forming a seal.

Men should follow one another out of the compartment at intervals of 15 or 20 seconds.

On reaching the surface, close the mouthpiece valve. Then the noseclip and mouthpiece may be removed. If the lung is to be used as a life preserver, fold over the flutter valve and clip it with a trouser clip. The lung may be re-inflated as necessary with the breath (but only for renewing its buoyancy when using it is a life preserver.)

The Following Precautions Should Be Kept In Mind When Making Ascents:
If for any reason it is impossible to breathe through the lung (mouthpiece knocked out of mouth, stuck valve) the ascent must be continued, as if using the lung, but exhaling slowly to relieve the pressure as the air in the lung expands.

If the noseclip comes off the nose, it may be replaced by using one hand while the other hand maintains a hold on the line, or the nose may be held with one hand. The man must never let go the line with both hands. If a man does let go the line with both hands he must back water to retard as much as possible his rate of ascent. If a shot of soda lime dust is drawn into the mouth (practically impossible with the latest types of lungs) it may be swallowed without harm. The tendency to cough, must, however, be stifled so the mouthpiece will not come out of the mouth.

Man Overboard:
Anyone seeing a man fall overboard shall pass the word in a loud clear voice toward bridge "Man overboard starboard (port) side."

Throw out life rings with torches attached.

Word will be passed from bridge "man overboard." Rig out bow planes. Men on deck with life jackets.

Men will stand by on deck with heaving lines and boat hooks. A good swimmer should be designated to stand by to go after man if he cannot assist himself.

Quartermaster and lookouts keep continuous watch on man and life buoys.

Ship will be handled by conning officer either by backing or circling to put bow planes near man in water. The bow planes can then be used as a working platform close to water. Men going out on planes should have lines attached to them.

Diving and surfacing are the two most fundamental procedures that make a submarine what it is. Here we see US Navy descriptions of how these procedures were performed according to textbook instructions aboard an S-class submarine. Yet in combat conditions, such routine actions might have to be heavily abbreviated according to the level of emergency. A good case in point is the "crash dive", an emergency dive performed when the submarine found itself under an immediate threat, typically when sighting an enemy aircraft or fast escort vessel making an attack run. In a standard dive procedure, the submarine would go through a rigorous sequential drill of preparation before submerging, sometimes taking several minutes to perform. In a crash dive, by contrast, a skilled crew could put the submarine underwater at break-neck pace, sometimes as little as 30 seconds, with the submarine actually starting to submerge even with crew still on the conning tower, frantically scrambling down and shutting the top hatch even as the water flooded in.

The Fleet Type Submarine (1946)

C. DIVING AND SURFACING PROCEDURES

20C1. Diving procedure.

A. Officer of the deck.
1. Pass the word, "Clear the bridge."
2. Check all hands below.
3. Sound two blasts on the bridge diving alarm as the last lookout passes the OOD.
4. When below, check report pressure in the boat and order the depth desired.
5. Commence attack, evasive tactics, or rig for depth charge as conditions warrant.

B. Quartermaster.
1. Be last down hatch and shut hatch.

C. Junior officer of the deck.
1. Be among the first down the hatch if on the bridge.
2. Proceed immediately to diving station.
3. Assume control of dive, carrying out procedure listed under control room.

D. Lookouts.
1. Clear the bridge on the double man diving stations in accordance with the Watch. Quarter, and Station Bill.

E. Conning tower talker watch.
1. Sound the general alarm if ordered by the OOD.
2. Lower the periscope if it is up.

F. Helmsman.
1. Put the rudder on as ordered; otherwise amidship.
2. Ring up full speed on the annunciators.

G. Maneuvering room.
1. Answer bells as ordered.
2. Shut the maneuvering room induction hull valve.

H. Engine room. Procedure in the engine room is carried out in this order
1. Stop the engines.
2. Shut the outboard exhaust valves.
3. Shut the engine and supply ventilation induction hull valves.
4. Shut the bulkhead flappers.
5. Shut the inboard exhaust valves.
6. If everything is in order in the engine rooms-oilers to control room-for submerged stations.

I. Control room.
1. Open the vents.
2. Rig out the bow planes and put them on 22-degree dive.
3. When all outboard exhaust valves are shut or when passing 23 feet shut the engine air induction and the ship's supply outboard valve.
4. Bleed air in the vessel and secure air on orders of the diving officer only in case the torpedo rooms do not bleed in air.
5. Note and report pressure in boat.
6. Put the stern planes on dive to take the ship to the ordered depth with a 4- to 6-degree angle.
7. Shut the bow buoyancy at 30 feet and open the safety for 5 seconds; then shut it. Shut all vents at 50 feet.
8. Blow the negative to 1,500 pounds in two steps.
9. Reduce the speed and adjust the trim as necessary.
10. Shut the negative flood and vent tank inboard.

11. Make certain that the periscopes are cut in.
12. When convenient, open all bulkhead flappers and resume normal hull ventilation.

J. Crew's mess.

1. Report the engine air induction and hull ventilation valves shut by hand signal to control room.
2. Lock the above valves shut as soon as possible and report to control.

K. All stations.

1. Shut the bulkhead flappers.

L. Forward torpedo room and after torpedo room.

1. Bleed air into the vessel and secure on word from the control room.

M. Radio room.

1. Disconnect the antenna lead and shut the trunk flapper.

The conning officer retains speed control at all times, However, this will not interfere with or necessitate any hesitation by the diving officer to request speed changes to facilitate depth control.

20C2. Surfacing procedure.

a. Duties of the officer of the deck.

1. Prior to surfacing, carry out surfacing routines as outlined in the front of the QM notebook.
2. Have the sound watch make an exacting search.
3. Keep the periscope watch as directed.
4. Give control any changes in ordinary surface procedure.
5. Pass the word, "Stand by to surface .... engine combination."
6. Follow the commanding officer and the quartermaster to the bridge. (The JOOD follows the OOD to the bridge.)
7. On surfacing, be prepared for immediate diving should circumstances warrant such action.
8. Upon proceeding to the bridge, the OOD takes the starboard side and searches, the JOOD takes the port side, and the QM the after half of ship. When all three have reported, "All clear," call to conning tower, "Routine."
9. When the word, "Routine" is passed, the officer in the conning tower sees that the following procedure is carried out:

a) Main induction opened.

b) Lookouts to the bridge.

c) Engines are automatically started on opening of induction.

d) Turbo blow for 6 minutes.

c) Gunner's mate to bridge to rig 20 mm.

f) Rig in soundhead if going two-thirds speed.

g) After steps a) to e) have been carried out, announce to control, "Carry out all routine below."

b. Helmsman.

1. When the surfacing alarm is sounded, ring up two-thirds speed unless otherwise ordered.

c. Quartermaster.

1. Stand by the hatch.

2. Sound the surfacing alarm on orders of the C.O. only.

3. Open the hatch on orders from the C.O.

d. Assistant navigator (quartermaster).

1. Keep the C.O. informed of keel depth and pressure in boat.

e. Control.

1. Start the hydraulic plant at 50 feet.

2. Rig in the bow planes when the word is passed to stand by to surface .... engine combination.

3. Blow the bow buoyancy and main ballast, except the safety, on the third blast of the surface alarm. Surface with 3-4 degree rise angle and secure the air when at 30 feet.

4. When the conning tower hatch shows a red light, and the hatch is heard to open, vent and flood the negative. Vent and shut the safety.

5. Open the main induction on orders from the conning tower.

6. Put the low-pressure blowers on tank as directed.

7. CPO of the watch: Carry out routine as directed. "Carry out all routine below" means:

a) Have the battery charge started.

b) Blow all the sanitary tanks.

c) Pump all the bilges in succession from aft to forward.

d) Assemble trash and garbage in control room.

c) Speed up the exhaust and supply blowers.

f) Start the air change after stopping the turbo blow.

g) Swab down and clean all compartments.

h) Report to the bridge that "All routine is being carried out below."

8. Be prepared to dive again immediately.

f. Crew's mess.

1. Unlock and put the hull ventilation supply and engine air induction valves on power, on "Stand by to surface." Report to control when this is accomplished.

g. Maneuvering room.

1. Answer bells as ordered. After the surface alarm is sounded, shift to surface rpm.

2. Ring up "Start" on the engines desired.

3. Shift to engines for propulsion when the engine room is ready and start the battery charge as soon as possible.

4. Report to the conning tower as soon as the battery charge is started.

h. Engine room.

1. When "Start" is received from the maneuvering room and when the outboard engine air induction valve is opened, start the engines as ordered, Carry out the normal routine.

20C3. Check-off list prior to surfacing.

a. Procedure 30 minutes prior to surfacing

1. Pump down the pressure in the boat to 0.1 inch upon orders of the C.O.

2. Start the hydrogen detectors and line up the battery ventilation for charge. Take individual cell reading.

3. Call the lookouts and have them dress appropriately for the weather.

4. Quartermaster: Clean all binoculars and get dressed to go to the bridge.

5. Bring .45-caliber pistol and submachine gun to the conning tower with two drums of ammunition.

6. Get readings on all sanitary tanks, bilges, and fresh water tanks and record them for final trim estimate.

7. Rig the curtain in the control room. Darken the control room and conning tower.

b. Procedure 15 minutes prior to surfacing.

1. Notify the maneuvering room and engine rooms to stand by engine combination in accordance with night orders.

2. Check to ascertain that all lookouts are in the control room dressed to go on watch with dark glasses.
3. Navigator: Relieve the OOD to get dressed for surfacing.
4. Diving officer on proceeding to watch: Relieve the diving officer to get dressed for surfacing and the JOOD watch.
5. Trim manifold man: Relieve the bow planesman to get dressed for surfacing.
6. Start up the SJ radar and have the radio technician man the SJ radar in the conning tower.

c. Procedure upon surfacing.
1. Immediately upon surfacing, stern planesman and trim manifold man go to the engine rooms.

Although a submarine commander's preference was to use deck guns if possible, the torpedo remained the principal tool for destroying enemy vessels. Torpedoes were, in themselves, highly complex pieces of equipment, requiring, much like the submarine itself, systems of propulsion, depth-keeping and steering but with the added complexity that they had to be fully automatic. Maintaining, readying and firing torpedoes was therefore a highly responsible job. This much is evident in the following passage from the 1943 manual *US Navy Torpedo Mark 18 (Electric): Description, Adjustment, Care, and Operation*. The Mk 18 torpedo actually entered production in 1943, as an improvement upon the US Navy's Mk 14 standard type, which had been plagued by technical unreliability, the problems including premature detonation, lack of detonation on impact (both these problems were caused by the problematic Mk 6 magnetic exploder), a tendency to run too deep and the occasional propensity to run in a circular pattern, which on occasions resulted in the destruction of the submarine – see the reference to the USS *Tang* above. The Mk 18 was a better prospect altogether. One of its advantages was that it was impelled by an electric motor, meaning that the torpedo did not leave behind it a wake of bubbles, which an enemy could use to trace back the torpedo path to the submarine that fired it.

US Navy Torpedo Mark 18 (Electric): Description, Adjustment, Care, and Operation (1943)

GENERAL DESCRIPTION

The Mark 18 is an electrically propelled torpedo. Propulsion power is supplied from a direct current series wound motor which receives its energy from an electric storage battery. The gyroscope and other control mechanism is air-driven similarly to that of the Mark 14 torpedo, except that the gyroscope is only subjected to an initial spin impulse and is of the "run down" type; the constant spin feature being made inoperative.

The Mark 18 is the first electric storage battery torpedo manufactured for the United States Navy and it is designed primarily for use as a submarine torpedo.

The complete torpedo is composed of the following units:

Warhead (or exercise head).
Battery compartment.
Afterbody including gyro and control mechanism.
Tail.

The designation Mark 18 applies to the complete torpedo and to the warhead, battery compartment, afterbody and tail; but the exercise head and the gyroscope have individual designations which are given over their respective descriptions.

PRINCIPAL DIMENSION, WEIGHTS AND CHARACTERISTICS
DESIGNATION MARKS OF PRINCIPAL PARTS

1. Torpedo	Mark 18.
2. Warhead	Mark 18.
3. Exploder	Mark 4 Mod. 2.
4. Detonator	Mark 8.
5. Booster	Mark 2.
6. Exercise head	Mark 34.
7. Exercise head air release mechanism	Mark 5.
8. Gyro	Mark 12 Mod. 3.

DIMENSIONS

Diameter	21″.
Length over-all with warhead	20′6″.
Length over-all with exercise head	20′6″.
Length of warhead to joint line	47.28″.
Length of exercise head to joint line (including towing eye)	47.28″.
Length of battery compartment joint line to joint line	125.90″.
Length of afterbody joint line to joint line	53.62″.
Length of tail end to joint line	19.19″.
Length forward end of guide stud to tail	141.438″.

GENERAL REMARKS

APPROXIMATE WEIGHTS

Explosive charge	600 pounds.
Warhead, empty without attachments	108 pounds.
Warhead loaded with exploder	736 pounds.
Exercise head, ready for run	736 pounds.
Battery compartment, without battery	395 pounds.
Three battery boxes, and battery assembly with acid	1,215 pounds.
Battery compartment, including battery	1,610 pounds.
Afterbody and tail cone complete with motor	694 pounds.
Ballast for exercise run	620 pounds.

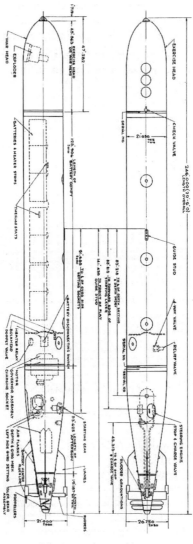

Mk 18 torpedo assembly.

| Torpedo, ready for war shot | 3,040 pounds. |
| Torpedo, ready for exercise shot | 3,040 pounds. |

BUOYANCY, TRIM, AND STABILITY

Displacement (water 1.024 specific gravity)	2,580 pounds.
Buoyancy, ready for war shot	-565 pounds.
Buoyancy, exercise head blown	+120 pounds.
Weight expelled (620 pounds of calcium chloride solution having a sp. gr. of 1.355).	480 pounds.
Center of buoyancy to end of tail	138.19 inches.
Center of gravity to end of tail (ready for war or exercise run)	140.19 inches.
Pull around	3,600 inch-pounds.

CAPACITY

| Air flasks (three flasks), total cubic inches | 630. |
| Air flask pressure, pounds per square inch | 2,800. |

POWER PLANT CHARACTERISTICS

Storage battery, rate	4.04 kilowatt-hour.
Open circuit battery voltage	168-172.
Motor, direct current, series wound (horsepower at 140 volts, 1,620 r. p. m.).	84 horsepower.
Motor speed	1,620 revolutions per minute.
Gear ratios, motor to propellers	1 to 1.
Forward propellers:	
Diameter	17.062 ± .062.
Pitch	Variable.
After propellers:	
Diameter	16.187± .062.
Pitch	Variable.
Propeller r. p. m. at 29 knots	1,620.
Pressure, air flasks working, pounds per square inch	3,000.
Pressure, reducing valve, low pressure, pounds per square inch	400.
Pressure, gyro nozzle, initial spin pounds per square inch	3,000.

RANGE CHARACTERISTICS

Normal power, acceptance, yards	4,000.
Normal speed, acceptance and service, knots	29.
Normal power, expected service, yards	4,000.

INTERCHANGEABILITY

All assembled units and mechanisms are interchangeable as such; and in general all detail parts are also interchangeable except for lapping, dowelling, etc. [. . .]

MARK 18 WARHEAD

DESCRIPTION

The warhead contains the explosive charge of "torpex"; the booster charge of tetryl; the detonator charge of fulminate of mercury and the firing mechanism, hereafter referred to as the exploder. The prime function of the torpedo is to carry the warhead to and explode it against an enemy vessel.

The warhead for the Mark 18 torpedo is designated as the Mark 18. The shell is made of sheet steel, ogival in form with the after section cylindrical. A steel joint ring is welded to its after end. This ring is tapped to receive the 20 steel joint screws for connecting the warhead to the battery compartment. The joint ring is also flanged to receive the dished steel bulkhead, which is secured to the joint ring by 49 steel studs, welded in the joint ring, and brass nuts. These hold the bulkhead in place over a rubber gasket forming a watertight seal at the after end. This watertight seal keeps the charge dry while in stowage. Sea water is kept clear of the bulkhead during a run by a soft rubber gasket inserted between the warhead joint ring and the forward battery compartment joint ring.

A steel nose piece in which a horizontal hole is machined for handling is welded to the forward end of the shell.

The warhead is fitted to receive a standard United States Navy exploder mechanism, Mark 4 Mod. 2. A steel flange is welded to the bottom of the

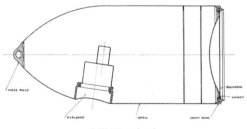

MK 18 warhead

shell to which in turn is welded a steel exploder casing. Extending from the top of this casing is a copper pocket for the tetryl booster. The exploder casing flange- has a machined seat that is drilled and tapped to receive the 12 studs by which the exploder base plate is secured.

The explosive charge consists of 600 pounds of "torpex" which partially fills the head. The tetryl booster Mark 2, containing about 7 ounces of compressed tetryl, is used in conjunction with the Mark 8 fulminate of mercury detonator.

The principal differences from other exploders are: The second modification of the Mark 4 exploder is to change the shape of the bottom plate for mounting on the new circular exploder base plate.

The Mark 8 detonator differs from the Mark 7 only in having a double thread between the detonator holder and safety chamber and a shorter arming time.

The joints of all parts attached to the shell are made watertight by welding, which is ground off flush on the outside edges.

All parts of the warhead and attachments are designed to withstand an external pressure of 135 pounds per square inch. Each empty warhead is subjected to an internal pressure of 5 pounds per square inch.

"Torpex" is an extremely stable explosive, but when detonated, a very powerful one. Its detonation is accomplished by the detonation of a small amount of tetryl, known as the booster. The booster is carried inside of the exploder casing on the upper part of the exploder mechanism. The booster is located approximately at the center of the explosive charge. The sequence of explosions is initiated when the firing pins of the exploder mechanism strike the Winchester caps and ignite the fulminate of mercury in the Mark 8 detonator. Fulminate of mercury is a very unstable explosive compound requiring the utmost care in transportation and handling. It is desirable to use only the smallest amount required to produce the desired results. Between the detonator and the "torpex" stands the comparatively safe tetryl booster, which can be detonated by a small amount of fulminate of mercury and which has sufficient power to detonate the "torpex."

The detonator is housed in a safety chamber where it can explode without setting off the booster, except when the exploder is in the fully armed position.

The tetryl booster is stored in a special stowage rack built into the warhead locker. The Mark 8 detonator carried by the detonator holder and assembled inside the safety chamber is stored as a unit in special watertight stowage boxes.

MARK 4 MOD. 2 EXPLODER-DESCRIPTION

Except for the base plate the Mark 4 Mod. 2 exploder is the same as the Mark 4 Mod. 1, description and tests of which are given in 0. P. 663. Brief descriptions of the base plate and transverse shaft not covered in 0. P. 663 follow.

THE BASE PLATE

The exploder is carried on a circular bronze base plate of suitable dimensions to fit into the base plate flange of the warhead. It is secured over a gasket by 12 holding screws. The impeller is completely housed within a channel cast in the base plate. Water is conveyed to the impeller through the forward end of this channel and is discharged through an extension of this channel on the after side of the impeller. A guard is secured in this channel directly under the impeller for the dual purpose of protecting the blades from damage, and conveying the water to the blades.

The impeller is of the open bucket type, composed of a hub to which 15 blades are permanently attached in casting. The impeller shaft passes through a square hole machined through the center of the impeller hub.

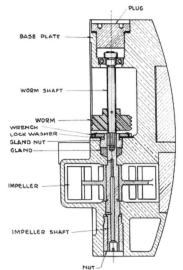

The impeller shaft is made of copper nickel alloy and is suitably machined for bearings in the channel on the base plate. The central portion is square to fit the square hole in the impeller hub. A hole is drilled longitudinally part way through the center of this shaft connecting with two radial holes in the wake of the gland bearing, affording a means of lubricating and grease sealing the impeller shaft. A hexagonal hole is machined in the driving end of the shaft for use in coupling to a transverse shaft.

After assembly of the shaft and the impeller in the base plate, the shaft is prevented from lateral movement in its bearings by a stop

Exploder mechanism. Section through impeller shaft.

plug screwed in place over its outer end. A hole is machined in this stop plug to facilitate the installation of a grease gun or the testing equipment. The inner end of the impeller shaft passes through a stuffing box in the base plate channel. The stuffing box crosshead is adjusted to prevent leakage of water, still maintaining a minimum friction on the shaft.

The castellated gland nut is secured by a special lock washer which maintains the proper tension on the packing gland. This also prevents loosening of the gland during transportation prior to firing-as well as during the run-and obviates the necessity of locking the nut with safety wire.

The transverse shaft is carried on one end in the machined end of the impeller shaft and on the other by a small commercial ball bearing, which rests in the outer flange of the base plate.

METHOD OF SECURING TRANSVERSE SHAFT

Keyed near the inboard end of the transverse shaft is a large worm which meshes with a worm wheel on the lower end of the vertical shaft. The lower end of the vertical shaft is carried in a bearing in the base plate, the upper end in the top plate of the exploder Mechanism. Near the upper end of the vertical shaft is a loose-fitting combination worm and pinion, positioned vertically by a steel pin pressed through the vertical shaft. This pin also keys the combination worm and pinion by engaging in two slots milled 180° apart on the lower end of the worm for the transmission of rotary motion. The worm meshes with a worm wheel on the horizontal shaft of the anticountermining device (which provides rotational motion tending to withdraw the anticountermining rack and fork from its "actuated" position); and the pinion meshes with another pinion carried on the lower end of a short shaft running through the exploder top plate. On the upper end of this short shaft is secured another small pinion meshing with an idler gear which in turn meshes with the arming gear on the exploder. This completes the transmission of motion from the impeller to the arming element.

CHAPTER 3
OPERATIONAL TECHNOLOGIES AND PROCEDURES

Submarines have by their very nature extremely limited visibility. During World War II, for most of their time submarines operated on the surface of the water, with crew on the conning tower using visual means, when relevant, to assist with navigation and tactical manoeuvring. When submerged, however, all visual reference was lost, apart from the periscope. Using the periscope presented some significant risks, because the submarine had to sit just under the surface of the water to deploy the scope, making it spottable, especially in clear waters or from an overhead aircraft. Furthermore, in smooth waters the periscope would cut a noticeable wake through the water, further giving away its position. In an immediate combat environment, therefore, a submarine would be heavily reliant upon hydro-acoustic means – essentially listening underwater – to detect and monitor surface shipping.

This chapter focuses on some of the unique operational procedures and technologies aboard a World War II submarine, beginning with the functions of a US sonar operator. The performance of this task must have demanded individuals with exceptional levels of concentration, levels that could be maintained amidst the danger and drama of a combat situation.

Submarine Sonar Operator's Manual (June 1944)

SONAR GEAR

SONAR is the name applied to all underwater sound gear. Like radar, it is a coined name, taken from the words SOund Navigation And Ranging.

When a submarine submerges, radar becomes useless and no lookouts remain on deck. The periscope and the sonar gear are now the eyes and ears of the submarine. But in the vicinity of enemy ships, it may be dangerous to use the periscope very often. Then the submarine must depend chiefly on listening. The sonar operators become the main channel of information about the maneuvers of the enemy.

Ships make sounds

Any ship moving through the water makes a certain amount of sound. Most important to the sonar operator is the sound of enemy propellers as they churn through the water. Next in importance to the sonar operator are the noises from various pieces of machinery within the ship. These sounds go through the hull and out into the water. With the ship stopped dead in the water, propellers and machinery may both be silent. But even then some sound may come from the slapping of the waves against the ship's hull.

The purpose of sonar gear is to detect these various sounds

Sonar listening gear has 5 essential parts

1. **Hydrophones.** On a modern submarine there are three hydrophones: one topside and two just below the level of the keel.

2. **Cables.** A cable runs from each hydrophone through the submarine's hull.

3. **Receiver-Amplifiers.** The other end of each cable is connected to a receiver-amplifier, which looks something like a radio.

4. **Headphones**. A pair of head phones can be plugged into the phone jack of each receiver-amplifier.

5. **Training Mechanisms.** Hand-operated and electrically controlled mechanisms turn the hydrophones in any desired direction.

The sounds made by a ship

are picked up when the hydrophone is trained in the ship's direction and are changed into electric currents which pass through a cable

to the amplifier where they are strengthened so that the sounds can be heard in the headphones.

The principles of sonar listening are simple

There are two main types:

Sonic gear picks up sound you could hear with your own ears if you stuck your head out into the water.

The Hydrophone in sonic gear resembles a long bar and is mounted topside, either port or starboard, forward of the conning tower.

The Amplifier at the other end of the connecting cable from the hydrophone is located in the forward torpedo room.

The Training Mechanism alongside the amplifier consists of a handwheel which turns the shaft on which the hydrophone is mounted. There is also a pointer and dial marked off in degrees.

JP is the Navy term for sonic listening gear. The *J* means that it can be used for listening only. The second letter *P* merely indicates the model of sonar listening gear.

Supersonic gear picks up sounds too high for the human ear to hear and changes them into sounds which can be heard.

The Two Hydrophones (Projectors) are mounted at the bottom of shafts, which extend through the hull under the forward torpedo room. Lowering these shafts puts the two projectors below the keel.

The Receiver-Amplifiers, one for each projector, are located in the conning tower. They look alike and they both operate in the same way.

The Remote-Control Units, one for training each projector, are also in the conning tower, on top of the receiver-amplifiers. Actually the projector shafts are turned in the forward torpedo room, by training mechanisms run by electric motors.

JK/QC is the Navy term for one type of supersonic gear. The *JK* half of the combination projector is for listening only; the *QC* half can also be used for sending out sounds into the water.

QB designates the other type. As indicated by the letter *Q*, the QB projector can send as well as receive sounds.

Comparison of sonic and supersonic listening

Since enemy ships make sonic and supersonic sounds, both types of gear are necessary for efficient listening. Each has its own particular advantages one is incomplete without the other.

Sonic gear is useful for picking up targets at great distances because sonic sounds travel farther. Also, on the JP gear sounds appear more natural and are more easily recognized. Therefore, you can identify not only the machinery noises of enemy ships, but also any telltale noises your own submarine is making.

Supersonic gear is useful for picking up the important supersonic noises that sonic cannot get. Supersonic gear is especially superior for catching the bursts of supersonic sound used by enemy escort vessels in searching for our submarines. (In addition, QB and QC gear can be used to send out sounds into the water to determine the range of an enemy ship.)

The WCA Installation

The WCA Installation on a submarine includes all the sonar gear that handles *supersonic* sounds. Much of this equipment is grouped in the conning tower, where it is known as the "WCA Stack." To locate all the various units, let us subdivide WCA into its two main parts:

QB Gear has its receiver-amplifier and remote-control unit in the conning tower. The projector is mounted on the starboard shaft and extends just below the keel under the forward torpedo room. The electric training mechanism for turning the projector is in the forward torpedo room.

JK/QC Gear also has its receiver-amplifier and remote-control unit in the conning tower, and its training mechanism in the forward torpedo room. The double-faced projector extends just below the keel on the port side, opposite the QB projector. A range indicator, used with either QB or QC, is also part of the WCA stack in the conning tower.

NOTE: The WCA Installation also includes NM gear (in the control room), which is used for determining the depth of the water beneath the keel.

BEARINGS: RELATIVE AND TRUE

A bearing is a number which tells the direction of another ship or object. A lookout gets bearings by sight, a conning officer by looking through the periscope, a sonar operator by listening through his gear. After contact is made with a target, the sonar operator keeps reporting bearings continually. Therefore, he has to know what bearings are, and how to read and report them.

Relative Bearings

Usually a sonar operator reports relative bearings because they tell direction in relation to own ship. Imagine two lines drawn from the center of the submarine: the first through the bow dead ahead, and the second to the target. The angle between these two lines, measured clockwise from the first line, is the relative bearing. A target dead ahead is at 000 degrees relative. Since there are 360 degrees in a circle, dead astern is at 180 degrees relative. These three diagrams show relative bearings of 50 degrees, 160 degrees, and 240 degrees.

True Bearings

The sonar operator may also be ordered to report a target's true bearing. Imagine two lines drawn from the center of the submarine: the first to the North Pole, the second to the target. The angle between them, measured clockwise from the first line, is the true bearing. A target due North of the submarine is at 000 degrees true, due East at 090 degrees true, due South at 180 degrees true, due West at 270 degrees true no matter where the submarine is heading. Only when own

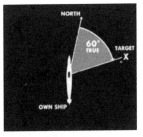

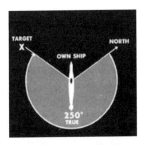

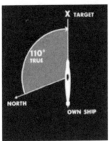

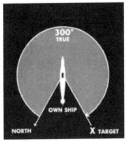

ship is heading due North, will a target's relative bearing and its true bearing be the same. Note how the true bearings are measured in the figures above.

Reading a bearing indicator

Below is a picture of a bearing indicator. It has three parts:

1. The outer scale represents relative bearings. Zero always points to your own submarine's bow.

2. The inner scale represents true bearings. Zero always points to true north, no matter where your submarine is heading.

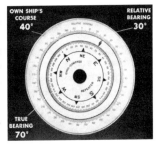

3. The diamond-shaped bug has two tips which point out on both scales the direction in which the projector is facing.

This is how to read the bearings

1. Read the relative bearing at the outer tip of the bug.

75

2. Read the true bearing at the inner tip of the bug.

NOTE: You can also read your own submarine's course on the true (inner) scale by noting the degrees directly below zero relative.

When own ship changes course
The diagrams below show that the relative bearing changes when own ship's heading changes. But the true bearing, measured from the motionless North Pole, is fixed. Therefore keeping the true bearing in mind helps the operator maintain contact with a target, no matter where his submarine is heading.

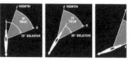

Know these general terms
The direction of a target may also be described in a more general way, as shown in the diagram at the right. Ahead, astern... port and starboard...bow, beam, and quarter...these are familiar words. But you must learn to know these eight combinations by heart, so that the instant you hear any one of them, you get a picture of the general direction of the target in relation to your submarine.

[. . .]

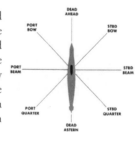

How sound waves behave in water

The behavior of sound waves in water is a rather complicated subject. Here are some of the most important features to remember.

Velocity
Sound waves travel very rapidly in water – about 4800 feet per second, as compared with 1100 feet per second in air. Weak sounds and strong sounds, high frequencies and low frequencies, all travel at the same speed. But their speed is affected by the temperature, pressure, and salinity of the water, as shown at the right.

Refraction
The fact that the speed of sound varies, especially with temperature, explains why sound waves are bent out of their normal paths. This bending is called refraction. Usually water is warmer near its surface than at lower depths. As shown in the diagram BOVE, the upper part of a sound wave in the warmer water travels faster than the lower part in the colder water. This makes the sound wave bend downward.

Transmission loss
The sound that reaches the hydrophone is very much weaker than it was when it left its source. Two main factors explain this loss during transmission.

1. **Spreading.** As a sound wave goes out from its source in all directions, it spreads over a larger and larger area. Thus a given amount of sound has to cover an increasingly large space, and it gets thinner and thinner.

2. **Attenuation.** This term covers the weakening of the sound from a number of other causes. As the water particles move back and forth in the compressions and rarefactions of sound waves, they rub against one another. Some of their original strength is used up in friction. Also, during their travel, sound waves may hit air bubbles, seaweed, fish, the ocean surface, or other obstacles. Some of the strength of the sound waves is absorbed by these obstacles; some is scattered in other directions so that it never reaches the hydrophone.

   Most important to sonar is the fact that attenuation is greater with higher frequencies. For this reason, supersonic sounds lose strength more quickly than sonic sounds and therefore cannot travel as far.

Sonic and supersonic sounds from ships
It has already been mentioned that submarines are equipped with sonic and supersonic listening gear. Both kinds are necessary to pick up all the sounds we are interested in hearing.

Propellers generate a wide band of sonic and supersonic frequencies. Consequently, they can be detected with either type of gear.

Ship machinery noises are mainly in the sonic range. Sonic listening is necessary, not only to catch these sounds from enemy ships, but also to locate and identify noises from your own submarine that might give you away to enemy escort vessels.

Enemy echo-ranging, that is, sound signals sent out by enemy escort vessels in searching for submarines, is supersonic, and can be heard clearly with supersonic gear.

Slapping of waves and the sounds of surf pounding on a beach are largely in the sonic range. This is also true of most sounds made by fish and marine animals.

Only with a combination of sonic and supersonic listening can we be sure of hearing all of these sounds.

[. . .]

JP Search Procedures

When you are on sonar watch, until you get a contact, your time will be spent in routine searching. To get the proper rate of sweep, you will have to turn the handwheel rapidly. When you take over the watch, you first carry out ...

Rapid search

1. From the bearing at which the hydrophone was left by the previous watch, sweep through 000 degrees and continue on to 180 degrees.
2. Then, reversing direction, sweep back around the full circle to 180 degrees. If no suspicious sounds are heard, shift to ...

Progressive search

Sweep forward two full turns of the handwheel and then one turn back. Continue up the same side, two turns forward and one turn back, until you have crossed the bow. Then train rapidly down the opposite side to 180 degrees. Reverse direction and train two turns forward, one back, two forward, one back, until you have crossed the bow again. Then train rapidly down the other side ... and so on. Continue this procedure for the duration of your watch, unless ordered to do otherwise.

These are some of the sounds you are likely to hear

Report these sounds

1. Enemy ships' propellers have rhythmic, swishing beats. PT boats whine and freighters chug.

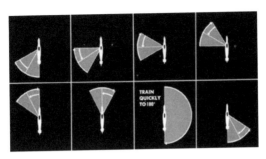

2. Enemy ships' machinery noise is not rhythmic like propellers. For example, generators sound just as you would expect.
3. Enemy echo-ranging (pinging) produces dull thuds or sometimes shrill peeps on JP.
4. On your own submarine, electric motors have a smooth hum; bow planes grate; the TDC whirrs; blowing tanks make a roaring sound.

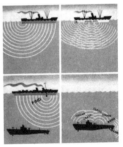

The only way to learn to know these sounds is to listen to them repeatedly on the JP training records. Every submarine has these records.

Learn to recognize these other sounds
1. Own ship's screws are heard at 180 degrees, except during silent running.
2. Shrimp snap; porpoise bark and whistle; drumfish sound like a drum; croakers croak.
3. The roaring pound of surf against a beach sounds quite natural.

Contact!

When your searching picks up a suspicious sound, your real job begins. The conning officer needs all the information you can give him. Here is what you must do – and do quickly.

1. Check the reciprocal bearing
Suppose you pick up a contact when the hydrophone is trained on 090 degrees. Immediately train halfway around the bearing circle to 270 degrees.

If the sound is weaker here, then you know 090 degrees is the correct contact bearing. But if the sound is stronger on 270 degrees, then 270 degrees is the right bearing to report, because the sound you heard on 090 degrees came through the baffle at the back of the hydrophone.

2. Report the contact

Immediately give the approximate bearing: "JP, contact, bearing ze-ro niner ze-ro." If you are not sure it is a ship, report: "JP, doubtful contact, bearing ze-ro niner ze-ro."

3. Adjust the amplifier controls

While you are reporting, set your amplifier controls to sharpen the target sound:

1. Set volume low enough to make the target distinct from the background noise.
2. Turn filter to the highest setting on which the target can still be heard.
3. As soon as you can hear on the 3000-cycle position, adjust the indicator control so that the magic eye just closes as the hydrophone is swung across the target.

4. Keep reporting accurate bearings

Make your eyes and ears work together. Use both the magic eye and the sound from your headphones to get the best bearings you can. Report every bearing you read. Keep adjusting your volume and filter controls to narrow the arc of the target.

5. Identify the target

As soon as possible, decide the probable kind of target. If it is a ship, notice the speed of the screws (slow, medium, or fast) and the weight of the sound (light or heavy). Report the nature of the target: "JP, bearing two eight eight. Sounds like a destroyer."

6. Keep information going to the conning tower

Get the turn count. Watch for any changes in the speed of the screws or in the loudness of the sound. Report every fact right away.

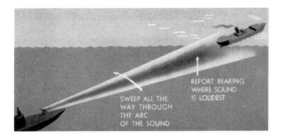

REPORT BEARING
WHERE SOUND
IS LOUDEST

SWEEP ALL THE
WAY THROUGH
THE ARC
OF THE SOUND

How to get accurate bearings

Read when sweeping from target's bow through target's stern
To get good bearings and to avoid losing contact, keep crossing the target. Sweep all the way through the screw noise. Then sweep back. Sweep all the way through again and all the way back. Determine which way the target is heading as quickly as possible. Then read the bearing only when sweeping in one direction: from the target's bow through the target's stern. Continue to sweep and to report bearings every time you cross the target in this one direction.

Read the bearing at maximum loudness
As you sweep across the target, the propeller noise increases to maximum loudness, and then dies away. There is also a change in the nature of the sound. Near the bearing of the propellers it has more of a hissing quality. With some experience, you will learn to combine the change in loudness and the change in quality to pick out the maximum point accurately.

If the sound is of equal loudness over a wide arc, proper use of the gain and filters will nearly always narrow it enough to give you a distinct maximum. Also, the more rapidly you sweep, the more noticeable the changes become – and the more accurately you can determine the peak.

Use the magic eye
The eye can be brought into operation as soon as you are able to listen on the 3000-cycle filter position. Adjust the indicator control until the eye just closes on each sweep through the target. Read the bearing the instant the eye closes. This should check with the bearing obtained by listening. Whenever you change the volume setting, you may have to reset the indicator control.

FLAT is a good position for searching because it permits you to hear all frequencies equally well.

BASS BOOST is good for listening to your own ship's noises, which are of low frequency.

500—If a contact is made on FLAT, shift to 500 as soon as you can. Change the volume if necessary.

3000—Shift to 3000 as soon as the target can be heard on this position. Again change the volume if necessary.

6000 is the best position for reading bearings. Use it as soon as possible in an approach.

Use volume and filters wisely

Low volume narrows the target

As soon as you get a contact, turn the volume control to the lowest setting at which the target can be heard. By cutting down the background noise level, this makes the propeller sounds stand out more clearly. With low volume, the arc of the target noise narrows. This allows you to get more accurate bearings.

Filters can define and narrow the target

Propeller noise is made up of all frequencies. But background noise, from the water and the submarine, is mostly low-frequency sounds. Therefore, by operating with a high-frequency filter you can get rid of the background noise, yet still hear the screws. Also at higher frequencies the target is heard over a narrower arc. So it is wise to use the highest filter setting on which the target can be heard.

How to take a turn count

1. Train the hydrophone directly on the bearing where the prop beats are loudest.
2. Turn the prop-count detector ON. It may bring out the beats more clearly. (If it does not, turn it OFF.)
3. Notice whether the beats are accented or unaccented. Accented beats go CHUG, chug, chug (three-bladed propeller) – or CHUG, chug, chug, chug (four-bladed propeller). Unaccented beats go chug, chug, chug, chug, chug.
4. Get in rhythm with the beats by pumping your arm up and down. If there is an accented beat, let your hand come down with every accented CHUG – or if the beats are all the same, on every chug.
5. Count the number of times you pump your hand down in 15 seconds.
6. Multiply this count by 4 to get the number of rpm (revolutions per minute). Report the rpm immediately. For example, if your 15-second count is 24, the rpm will be 96, and you will report: "JP, turn count is ze-ro nines six. Good count." If the beats are so rapid that you are not sure of the accuracy of your count, report: "Poor count."
7. After you have reported, make sure that the prop-count detector switch is OFF.

During approach and attack

Give the conning officer every scrap of information you can about the target. Be alert to catch and report:
. . . if it changes its course, turn count, or pinging rate.
. . . if it crosses your own bow or stern.
. . . if another ship comes between you and the target.
. . . if you lose contact.

Listen carefully to all orders from the conning officer. He may direct you to track the target. Or he may tell you to continue searching all around to keep in touch with the escort vessels in the screen, while another sonar operator stays on the target. If he fires torpedoes, he may order you to track them-to give bearings continuously on their whining sound as they run, and to report the crash as they explode.

During evasive maneuvers

In escaping from the enemy, the JP gear is frequently used to keep track of the attacking ship. Because of its topside mounting it can be operated even when you are lying on the bottom. It is also valuable for detecting telltale noises your own machinery may be making, using the bass-boost filter to bring out the low frequencies. If a doubtful sound remains on the same bearing when your own ship changes course, it is almost certainly from your own machinery. You should study our own ship's sounds so that you learn to recognize them quickly.

After depth charges – remagnetize

If depth charges are dropped near you, you probably will have to remagnetize the hydrophone. Plug the cable into the magnetizer jack, and press the push-to-magnetize button just once. Then plug the cable into the hydrophone jack and listen. If you cannot hear anything, magnetize the hydrophone again. Continue this procedure until the hydrophone is able to pick up sounds.

Securing JP gear

As soon as your submarine surfaces, secure the JP gear,

1. Turn the power switch off.

2. Train the hydrophone to 090 degrees if it is installed on the port side, or to 270 degrees if it is on the starboard side.

3. Hang up the headphones carefully. They are a special kind that cannot be replaced while you are on patrol. Other headphones do not work as well on JP gear.

Enemy echo-ranging

If in searching you hear the dull thuds or shrill peeps of enemy pinging (echo-ranging), quickly check the reciprocal bearing, and then report the approximate bearing of the pinging immediately. Estimate the time between pings. If it is over 2 seconds, report "long scale." If it is definitely less than this, report "short scale." Be alert to catch and report any change in the pinging rate.

The *Submarine Trim and Drain Systems* manual might appear as a particularly arcane volume to include in this book. And yet, as the first few paragraphs of this passage suggest, mastering the principles of trimming the submarine were utterly central to the proper movement of the vessel through the water, especially when submerged. In conditions of neutral buoyancy – where the submarine's average density is equal to the density of the fluid in which it is immersed – a submarine is inherently unstable. By adjusting the volume of water in the trim tanks positioned fore and aft of the submarine, the submarine is given a stable attitude in the water, assisted by the hydrodynamic effects of the controllable planes. Adjusting the trim was a skilled job, and requiring a steady hand and intelligent mind to do well. The following passage explains the core principles of the trim system, and how it was structurally arranged in wartime US submarines.

Submarine Trim and Drain Systems (1946)

INTRODUCTION
A. BASIC PRINCIPLES
1A1. Balance and stability. A modern submarine is designed to dive or surface rapidly under complete control. It must be able to proceed on the surface and to submerge at the desired rate of speed to the depths required. To do so quickly and efficiently, the submarine must maintain fore and aft balance, and athwartship stability. The chief function of the trim and drain system is to maintain this fore and aft balance by controlling the amount and distribution of water in the various tanks used for this purpose.

Before proceeding with the functional description of the trim and drain system, let us consider the factors affecting the balance and stability of the submarine. The balance and stability of the submarine are maintained by applications of the principles of buoyancy and the law of the lever.

1A2. Buoyancy. Buoyancy is the force which tends to keep an object afloat in water or any other liquid. When an object is immersed in a liquid, the liquid exerts pressure from all directions on the external surface of the object. The deeper the object is immersed in the liquid, the greater is the pressure exerted against its surface. Also, the upward pressure exerted by the liquid against the lower surface of the object is greater than the downward pressure against its top. If the immersed object weighs more than the liquid it displaces, it is said to have negative buoyancy. Such an object sinks. If the object weighs less than the liquid it displaces, the object is said to have positive buoyancy. Such an object floats, or if it is thrust under the surface of the liquid, it rises. When both the object and the liquid it displaces weigh the same, the object is said to have neutral buoyancy. If such an object is submerged, it remains submerged unless it is acted upon by an outside force.

1A3. Fore and aft balance. The conditions of positive, neutral, and negative buoyancy just described apply to sub-marine operations. However, these buoyancy conditions must always be considered with respect to the law of the lever, or the balancing of forces, on each side of the center of gravity of the boat. This is known as fore and aft balance. When a submarine is on the surface, or when it reaches a desired depth, the first objective is to attain perfect, or nearly perfect, trim, that is, a balancing of the forces. The trimming of the boat is accomplished by varying, or adjusting, the amount of water in the variable ballast tanks. The trim system is the means by which this adjustment is made.

B. TRIM SYSTEM

1B1. Functions. The assumption is made in the next few paragraphs that the submarine is in diving trim on the surface. The submarine is so designed that when the main ballast tanks are empty, it has positive buoyancy and can cruise on the surface. When the main ballast tanks are flooded, the positive buoyancy is destroyed, and a state of neutral buoyancy exists. This enables the submarine to cruise underwater at any desired depth. Of course, diving, surfacing, and cruising submerged are further controlled by means of the bow and stern planes and rudder and speed adjustments. However, the trim has been so carefully adjusted that by flooding the main ballast tanks and adding the required amount of water to the special ballast tanks, the submarine can be made to submerge at the desired rate.

In actual operation the condition of fore and aft balance assumed in the preceding paragraph is obtained by the use of the trim system. The trim system consists of a trim pump, a trim manifold, and the connecting piping leading to the variable ballast tanks. The trim system admits additional water ballast to the variable ballast tanks to compensate for loss of weight, removes water ballast to reduce excessive weight, and distributes water ballast to the proper tanks to compensate for unequal distribution of weight aboard the submarine.

For example, if additional stores are stowed in the forward end of the boat, water is pumped out of the forward trim tank and auxiliary tanks in accordance with the compensating sheet, to compensate for this additional weight. The auxiliary ballast tanks, No. 1 and No. 2 amidships, generally are used to compensate for over-all weight changes, and therefore water ballast must be taken into these tanks or discharged overboard as required.

Since the auxiliary tanks form a U outside the pressure hull and are separated at the keel, it follows that if a large amount of water ballast is added,

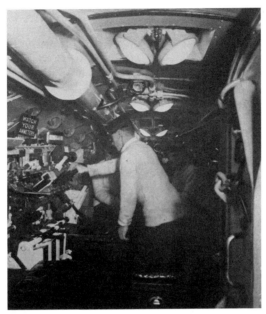

An engineer controls the main motors of a British submarine as the vessel submerges.

it must be added equally on both the port and starboard sides in order to prevent listing. Again, as in maintaining fore and aft balance, the trim system is used in adjusting the distribution of this water ballast so that athwartship stability is maintained. Either the port or the starboard tank may be used individually to correct listing of the ship.

The safety and negative tanks can be used as additional variable ballast tanks since they can be flooded and pumped by means of the trim manifold. In addition, the trim system can be used to flood and pump the water round torpedo (WRT) tanks, both forward and aft.

1B2. Standby trim pump. Because of the importance of the functions of the trim system, it is necessary that a standby trim pump be provided to insure operation of the system in the event of failure of the trim pump. This standby equipment is provided by cross connecting the drain pump of the drain system with the trim manifold of the trim system. Thus each pump serves as a standby for the other, assuring operation of both systems.

Another US manual (the US Navy was especially productive in its publishing and distribution of military instruction documents), *Standard Submarine Phraseology* represents something of a contrast to the extract above. Instead of engineering technicalities, this manual focused on the precise use of language aboard an operational submarine. Much like the importance of standardised language in air-traffic control today, submarines required a consistent and unambiguous system of communication between officers and men that provided the most direct links between words, comprehension and action. To those who have never served in the navy, the prescriptive nature of the phrasing might seem extreme. Yet in action, such brusque phrasing was essential. It reduced the time taken to convey combat information, plus made it easier for crew to understand what was being said amidst noise and chaos, through their recognising familiar patterns of speech. Thus mastering the language used was as important as mastering the equipment.

Standard Submarine Phraseology (c. 1943)

VOICE PROCEDURES

1. Components of a message

The typical message on a submarine consists of call and text. The call is the name of the station being addressed. The text is the body of the message. For example:

After room, open the outer doors.

(call)   (text)

In the rare cases when the source of a message is not obvious from the text, the identifying name of the sending station should be inserted following the call. For example: "Control, forward room, we heard a bumping noise along the hull."

The call is normally used because it serves the double purpose of alerting the correct listener and of helping to define the contents of the message. It should be omitted only when speed is essential and when the text of the message clearly indicates to whom it is addressed. For example: Rig for depth charge.-

2. Acknowledgments

Every message is acknowledged, but the method of acknowledgment varies with the type of message, as follows:

(a) Orders

Orders addressed to an individual or to a single compartment are acknowledged by repeating them back word for word. This repetition serves as a check on the accuracy of the reception of the order, and passes the word for action to other men in the compartment.

(Order)   **Forward room, set depth one ze-ro feet.**
(Acknowledgment) **Forward room, set depth one ze-ro feet.**

Orders addressed to all compartments are acknowledged from forward aft by giving the name of the compartment and adding "aye".

(Order)   **All compartments, secure from depth charge.**
(Acknowledgment) **Forward room, aye.**
                     Battery forward, aye. Etc.

(b) Reports

When the correct reception of its details is important, the report is repeated back word for word.

(Report)   **JP, contact, bearing two one ze-ro.**
(Acknowledgment) **JP, contact, bearing two one ze-ro.**

When a report of a routine nature is heard directly by the person to whom it is addressed, "Very well" or "Aye, aye" is usually sufficient acknowledgment.

(c) Questions

When a question can be answered immediately, the answer in itself constitutes an acknowledgement. The answer should be worded so that it is clear that the question has been understood.

(Question)   **Forward room, how are your bilges?**
(Answer)   **Control, forward room bilges are dry.**

When a question cannot be answered immediately, the immediate acknowledgment is normally a repetition of the question and the word, "Wait". For questions of a routine nature, "Aye, aye," plus "Wait" is usually sufficient acknowledgment. In either case, the answer is given as soon as the information becomes available.

(Question)	**Forward room, how are your bilges?**
(Acknowledgment)	**Forward room, how are your bilges? Wait.**
(Answer)	**Control, six inches of water in forward room bilges.**

3. Correction or change in a message

If the sender makes a mistake in giving a message, he says "Belay that" and gives the correct form.

> **Gyros forward, set gyros by hand ze-ro ze-ro fo-wer. Belay that.**
> **Set gyros by hand ze-ro fo-wer fo-wer.**

If the receiving station repeats a message incorrectly, the sender says "Belay that" and gives the correct message again.

4. Reports Of Execution

When an order has been carried out, this fact is reported to the station originating the order. Generally, the report of execution closely follows the wording of the order.

(Order)	**After room, open the outer doors.**
(Acknowledgment)	**After room, open the outer doors.**
(Report)	**Conning tower, the outer doors have been opened aft.**

Other common forms in reports of execution involve the phrases "has the word" and "on his way."

(Order)	**Tell Mr. R. to check the gun access hatch.**
(Report)	**Mr. R. has the word.**
(Order)	**Gunner's mate to the bridge.**
(Report)	**The gunner's mate is on his way.**

Certain special forms are given later in this manual.

5. Request for a repeat

If the receiver fails to understand any part of a message, he says "Repeat". The sender then gives the entire message again.

(Message) **JP, pick up target bearing wuh wuh nay.**
(Reply)   **Repeat.**
(Message) **JP, pick up target bearing one one eight.**

6. Emergency messages
In case of an emergency, the station making the announcement calls:

Silence on the line.

All other stations cease talking immediately until the word "Carry on" is received. If any message was interrupted by the emergency announcement, it is then repeated in full.

7. Station tests
A station test is conducted whenever a circuit is newly-manned, or when there is some question whether particular stations have been manned, and also at hourly intervals during each watch. The nature of the test is indicated by the following example:

(Order)   **All compartments, control testing.**
(Reports) **Forward room, aye.**
            Battery forward, aye.
            Conning tower, aye. Etc.

The stations answer in order from forward aft. If any station does not reply within five seconds, the next station comes in. The station passed over then enters at the end of the list.

Below are the correct station names on communication circuits. These particular names have been selected on the basis of tests which showed them to be the most easily understood and the least readily confused.

Forward room   Gyros forward
Battery forward   Gyros aft
Control   TDC
Conning tower   Bridge
Battery aft   Forward capstan
Forward engine room   After capstan
After engine room   Deck gun
Maneuvering   JP
After room

8. Shifting phones

A change of talkers at a telephone station during a watch is reported to the control station by the talker being relieved. The change of phones is made as soon as the report has been acknowledged. The new talker then reports his presence on the line. The control station may be either the control room or the conning tower.

(Report)	**Control, forward room shifting phones.**
(Acknowledgment)	**Control, forward room shifting phones.**
(Report)	**Control, forward room back on the line.**

9. Securing phones

Typically, phones are secured on receipt of an order from the control station.

(Order)   **All compartments, secure phones.**
(Reports) **Forward room, securing phones.**
          Battery forward, securing phones. Etc.

Phones are never secured without permission from the 00D. In special instances, it may be necessary to ask permission to secure.

> **Control, permission to secure phones in battery aft.**

After the permission is granted, the station reports that it is securing.

10. Frequently-used terms

The following terms, which are common to a number of commands, are used to avoid confusion and misunderstanding.

(a) **"Section one," "Section two,"** and **"Section thuh-ree."**
    "First section" sounds too much like "third section".
(b) **"Shut."**
    "Close" is often mistaken for "open" or blow".
(c) **"Shoot"** in preliminary commands.
    "Fire" is used only when giving orders to open fire.
(d) **"Permission to ..."** as a standard request before beginning an operation requiring special permission. For example: "Permission to start an air charge." "Granted."
(e) **"Man"** and **"secure",** as applied to various types of equipment.

11. Numerals in messages

The pronunciation of numerals as shown at the right is now standard for all the services. The numeral "0" is spoken as "ze-ro" except in giving ranges. For ranges, it is called "oh". When "00" occurs at the end of a range, it is called "double-oh". "000" at the end of a range is called "oh double-oh". "0000" at the end of a range is called "oh oh double-oh". Other rules for the use of numbers in messages are as follows:

ZE-RO
WUN
TOO
THUH-REE
FO-WER
FI-YIV
SIX
SEVEN
ATE
NINER

(a) Courses and bearings are spoken as three separate digits. (All bearings are understood to be relative unless followed by the word "true")

Steer course two fi-yiv fo-wer.

Bearing ze-ro ze-ro six.

Bearing one fi-yiv fo-wer, TRUE.

(b) Speed, depth to keel, and torpedo depth are spoken as two separate digits.

Speed ze-ro six knots.

Six fi-yiv feet.

Set depth at one two feet.

(c) Angle-on-the-bow is spoken as an ordinary compound number, preceded by 'port' or 'starboard'.

Angle-on-the-bow, port thirty fi-yiv.

(d) Angle of the boat and planes are spoken as ordinary compound numbers.

Two degree up angle, twenty degree rise on the bow planes.

(e) Time is given in standard Navy terminology.

Ze-ro ze-ro thirty.

Seventeen thirty fi-yiv.

Ze-ro eight hundred.

12. Brevity

Messages are given in standard form whenever possible, and are always kept brief. Words like "please", "sir", and "thank you" are not used on interior communication circuits.

BATTLE STATIONS
GUN ACTION

Typical orders used in battle stations gun action are given below. The detailed content of some of these will vary with the circumstances, but the general phrasing should remain the same.

From	Over Orders	
CO	1MC	**Battle stations gun action. Deck gun only.**
Gunnery officer	XJA	**Battery aft, fill the ammunition train.**
		When ammunition train is filled, battery aft reports this fact to the gunnery officer.
Gunnery officer	7MC	**Gunnery officer ready.**
CO	7MC	**Target is small sampan, bearing one two ze-ro, range fi-yiv oh double-oh.**
CO	7MC	**Stand by for battle surface.**
		For surfacing phraseology see page 24.
CO	7MC	**Open gun access hatch. Gun crew on deck.**
CO	1JP	**Deck gun commence firing.**
Gun captain		**Ready one. Fire one. Check fire.**
		Range fo-wer six double-oh. Scale fi-yiv eight. Resume fire.
		In an emergency any man may call: "Silence!"
		After the emergency is over the gun captain says: "Carry on."
CO	1JP	**Cease firing. Secure the deck gun. Clear the deck.**
		Last man down reports: "Gun access door shut."
CO	1MC	**Secure from battle stations.**

BATTLE STATIONS TORPEDO

The phraseology for battle stations torpedo is the same, whether the submarine is submerged or surfaced. For clarity, the following examples are arranged in three divisions according to the units receiving the orders.

To all compartments over 1MC

Battle stations torpedo.
XJA and JA talkers in conning tower conduct a station test.

Tracking party, man your stations.
This order is used as an alternative to the first when it is desired to track the target without manning all battle stations. Communication among members of the tracking party takes place over 7MC, plus any auxiliary circuits which have been set up linking conning tower, plot, radar, and sonar.

Rig for depth charge. (Over XJA)
When all compartments have reported rigged for depth charge, the conning tower talker- reports this fact.

Secure from battle stations. Section one take the watch.

To gyro regulators over JA

Gyros forward, match gyros by hand.

Gyros aft, shift to automatic.

Gyros forward, stand by to check gyros . . . Mark!
  Reports from gyros forward would be:
  Standing by . . . Thuh-ree fo-wer ze-ro.

Gyros forward, shift to hand. (in case of casualty)

Gyros forward, set gyros on thuh-ree fi-yiv six.

To torpedo talkers over XJA

Forward room, order of tubes is one, two, thuh-ree, fo-wer.
Forward room, make ready the forward tubes.
After room, except for opening the outer doors, make ready the after tubes.
Forward room, set depth ze-ro eight feet.
After room, open the outer doors on tubes seven and eight.
Forward room, stand by. Fire one. Fire two. Fire thuh-ree.

After receiving the report from the forward room that these tubes have been fired, the conning tower talker reports this fact to the approach officer.

Reload tubes one, two, thuh-ree.

This order is followed by a series of reports:

> **Conning tower, commencing reload forward.**
> **Conning tower, torpedo entering number one tube.**
> **Conning tower, reload completed on number one tube.**

When all designated tubes have been reloaded:

> **Conning tower, reload completed forward.**

After room, secure the after tubes.

For emergency firing

Emergency torpedoes forward.

When outer doors are open, forward room reports:

Conning tower, tubes one, two ready.

Fire one. Fire two.

CHAPTER 4

OFFENSIVE ACTIONS – TORPEDO AND GUNNERY ATTACKS

This chapter, and that which follows, is dominated by one source in particular, the invaluable *U-boat Commander's Handbook*. This extensive German handbook, published in 1942 but with an updated edition in 1943 (from which the extracts here are taken), was translated by the US Department of the Navy in the later years of the war. Although we should always allow for human adaptations to the realities of combat, rather than the slavish following of manual advice, the *U-Boat Commander's Handbook* is one of the best documents available for understanding submarine tactics in World War II.

In this chapter, we look specifically at offensive action, the tactics by which the U-boat commander would engage enemy vessels effectively either by gun or torpedo. During World War I, it was not uncommon for submarines to sink unarmed and unescorted merchant ships by deck gun alone. Such actions meant that the submarine could retain the speed advantage of surface running (World War II submarines could often do more than 20 knots per hour on the surface, but generally fewer than 10 knots when submerged), plus it was better to draw on the plentiful supply of gun shells, rather than the limited number of torpedoes. During World War II, however,

Seven members of a U-boat crew parade on deck as it sails away from port.

the heavier presence of escort vessels and anti-submarine aircraft meant that most attacks were carried out via torpedo when submerged. The nature of individual attacks somewhat depended on the skill and attitude of the commander. The best route to a confirmed kill was often to get in close, ideally to under 1,000yds (914m), which in some circumstances might mean a plucky commander actually taking his submarine into the heart of an enemy convoy. But long-range kills were also attempted and achieved, typically in the region of 2,500–4,000 yds (2,286–3,657m) but sometimes further, although at the extreme end of a torpedo's range a hit was as much a matter of luck than judgement. For most of the submarine crew, the only indicator of a hit would be a rumbling underwater boom and a euphoric shout from the captain.

U-boat Commander's Handbook (1943)

SECTION II
The Underwater Torpedo Attack
A. Fundamental Rules for the Underwater Attack.
91.) The object of the underwater attack is to discharge a torpedo with the certainty of hitting, but without warning, and at short range. The shorter

the distance between the submarine and the target, the more reliable the assessment of the speed, course, and position of the enemy. The torpedo attack at short range is the most advantageous also because not even important miscalculations affecting the launching of the missile can take effect to any appreciable extent, on account of the short course of the torpedo, and by reason of the fact that any counter-action on the part of the enemy – for example, a change of course (evading), if the submarine or the torpedo is spotted – comes too late.

92.) The lower limit of the torpedo attack at close range is defined by the distance needed to set the torpedo on its course at the appropriate depth, and by the safety interval, i.e., the distance of the submarine from the point of detonation of the torpedo. No torpedo attack should, therefore, be carried out at a range under 300 m.

93.) Invisibility during the attack is made possible by the judicious, invisible use of the periscope, the surgeless launching of the torpedo, and the absence of bubbles in the track of the torpedo.

94.) The efficiency of the sound-locating and ASDIC equipment of the enemy is dependent on the state of the sea, the nature of the water (i.e., conditions of "stratification," etc.), the speed of the enemy, the attentiveness of the personnel, and other factors. The danger to be anticipated from the sound location and ASDICs of the enemy should not be allowed to prevent the carrying out of a fatal attack at short range.

95.) When attacking ships with low and medium speeds, at close range, it is ballistically advantageous to fire at an angle of the target of 90, as errors estimating the position will in this case have the least effect, besides which the speed of the enemy can be most accurately gauged in this position. If the range is longer (over 1,000 m), and the target is traveling at a high rate of speed, an attempt should be made to launch the torpedo at a smaller angle, say, 60.

96.) The method of carrying out the attack is based, as long as range finding with subsequent deflection (change of bearing) measuring (keeping the reckoning) is not practicable, on the particulars of the enemy characteristics obtained by the viewing method during the preparation of the underwater attack, or on the estimates of the enemy characteristics obtained underwater: position, speed, range. The estimation of the characteristics of the target from the level of the submarine, and with the aid of the monocular optical system of the periscope, is difficult, and requires continual thorough practice.

97.) The estimation of the position is easiest when the submarine stations itself forward of the beam. If the sun is behind the target, the assessment of the position is difficult.

98.) The speed of the enemy can best be calculated from the position forward of the beam. In calculating the speed, attention should be paid to the water at the stern rather than to the sea near the bows, because, if the shape of the bows is narrow (pointed), the visible effect of the progress of the ship is often very slight. In addition, it is more difficult to camouflage the stern (i.e., so as to create the impression of movement, etc.).

In estimating the enemy's speed, his course in relation to the direction of the waves, as well as the change of bearing, should be taken into consideration.

99.) Every available opportunity should be taken of practicing range finding (i.e., estimating the range). In estimating ranges, conditions of visibility play an important part. In clear weather, and with the sun behind one's back, the distance is liable to be underestimated, in poor visibility, against the sun, in conditions of twilight (dusk and dawn), and by moonlight, to be overestimated.

100.) Favorable conditions for attack.

a) With the sun behind: The torpedo control officer is not dazzled, but can clearly see the sharp outline of the target. From the enemy ship, the periscope, raised no more than is absolutely necessary, is not to be seen among the reflections of the bright sun in the water; and also a trail of bubbles can not usually be seen until it is too late.

b) From the weather side (windward). The periscope should move with the sea. The waves, coming from behind, always wash over a periscope which is in the right position, that is to say, in a low position; and the splashes and spray water of the periscope are not easily made out. In addition, the enemy look-out to windward, especially in a strong wind, or in heavy rain, meets with difficulties.

As regards the weather side (windward), if the wind is moderate, torpedoes discharged from the stern form an exception (i.e., to the above inasmuch as the submarine, In moving with the waves (that is, in this case to leeward) comes near to riding on the waves, whereas to windward – driving against the sea – the periscope may cause conspicuous splashes even when the submarine is traveling at low speed. In a keen wind, however, the windward side is also more favorable for the stern launching of torpedoes, because the enemy, as a matter of course, then keeps a better lookout to leeward, and observation is better.

c) Wind 3 to 4 and sea 2 to 3 are most favorable for making the attack, because the sea then washes over the low-lying periscope, without interfering with the view of the target, while the action of the underwater (depth) steering gear is not adversely affected.

101.) Unfavorable conditions for attack.

a) Heavy seas or swell: It is difficult to keep the submarine at the right depth for attack, especially when the attack has to be carried out against the sea. According to the qualities (efficiency) of the underwater steering gear of the boat, this will soon put a limit to the possibilities of underwater attack (see Section I, D, No. 78). It is in a rough sea that an attack in a direction parallel to the waves is more likely to succeed most favorable for the underwater steering of the submarine and the depth course of the torpedo).

b) Sea as smooth as oil: The slightest ripple even of the low periscope is noticeable, and easily observable by the enemy. Exceptions: enemy coming out of a bright sun; conditions of twilight; moonlit nights.

c) Attack with dark thunderclouds in the background; even the most efficiently camouflaged (painted) periscope will then appear white against e dark black clouds.

d) Against the sun: the estimation of speed, position and distance (range) is considerably more difficult; besides which, if the attack is carried out against the sun, there is the danger of attracting attention by the flashes of light proceeding from the objective (lens system of the periscope).

[. . .]

B. Preparing for the Underwater Attack.

105.) General rules for the attack.

a) The submarine commander should be alert and suspicious on patrol, as long as there is no target; but everything should be thrown into the attack.

b) Proceed with care when a target has been found. The attack should be carried out with indomitable resolution and steadfastness, until final success, resulting in the annihilation of the enemy, has been achieved. During the attack, situations often arise which would be a reason for disengaging from the enemy. These moments of doubt, and these temptations, must be conquered.

c) Never delude yourself by assuming that it is right not to attack on the instant, or not to hold on the enemy with the utmost determination, because there may be reason to hope and believe that a better target will subsequently be found elsewhere. What you have got, you have got. Do not let such considerations give you the idea of trying to save fuel.

d) The attack should only be postponed in case of imperative necessity, for example at dusk – if it should already be too dark for underwater torpedo launching – in order to be able to carry out a surface attack after night-fall, with greater safety and a better chance of success.

e) In every submarine attack, whether by day or by night, the attempt must be made to obtain reliable data for aiming (controlling) the torpedo, by exhausting all possibilities with care and deliberation (measuring the deflection with the aid of the line (of the horizon), increase the size of the masts at a given height in the 1/16 scale, overhauling as to course and speed, by day and night, on the surface).

Do not attack immediately at random; success cannot be achieved that way.

f) Do not attack from positions which offer no chance of success. Keep your head and wait, in order – in daytime, if it is still light enough – to make a second attack by another overhauling maneuver, or in order to attack at night.

g) Particularly difficult objectives for the submarine are: destroyers, on account of their speed and the relative shortness of the target they offer, and submarines, on account of their small height (difficulty of range finding), and their shape above water, which is unfavorable for estimating their position. Consequently, attacks on destroyers and submarines can only be carried out at short range. No single shots; "fan" shooting.

h) In wartime, one is always farther away from the enemy than one thinks, especially at night. Hold out, then; and go near.

Firing at close range also makes for greater safety for your own boat. In the neighborhood of its own ships the enemy escort will not at first drop depth charges.

106.) As a matter of principle, every underwater attack should be so prepared and carried out that the launching of torpedoes can take place at the earliest possible moment. Favorable opportunities of attack may be lost by hesitating. If conditions allow, the submarine should therefore go to meet the enemy. It is wrong to keep ahead of the enemy and wait until he comes into range.

107.) The commander must be quick, resolute and versatile, and be guided by circumstances in deciding which method of attack is the most favorable, and will most quickly achieve success. As long as the enemy is in range, the submarine must be in a position to launch a torpedo at any moment, in case the enemy takes counter-measures, by veering, etc., even if the desired position most favorable for launching the attack, for example, an angle of 90, has not yet been reached. The commander should never concentrate rigidly and schematically on a certain desired position, and operate with that exclusive object in view.

108.) On account of the low underwater speed of the submarine, a position forward of the beam of the enemy is a necessity when making the underwater attack proper. The initial position for the underwater attack must be the more forward of the enemy's beam, the greater the distance is between the submarine and the enemy. In normal visibility and normal conditions of attack, the submarine should therefore not dive for the underwater attack until it has reached the position 0 in relation to the general course of the enemy.

109.) If the submarine is not already ahead of the enemy's beam when the latter comes in sight, an attempt must be made to reach the required position at top speed on the surface. The most favorable converging course in relation to the enemy when overhauling, is always the course vertical to the sight bearing, as long as the submarine is in a more forward position than abreast of the enemy.

110.) In taking up its station forward to the beam of the enemy, the submarine must not endanger its most valuable asset, invisibility. In daytime, in clear weather, the submarine should not therefore be able to see more of the enemy than just the tops of his masts (look-out on the mast, range-finder in the foretop).

111.) Attention should be paid to the differences in the conditions of visibility of the various sea areas. Conditions can be encountered in which it is possible to approach much nearer to a surface ship, without immediately being spotted, because the air is not always absolutely clear, and the dip of the horizon is frequently blurred and misty. In the Atlantic, a submarine can be spotted by the enemy as soon as it is lifted by the swell of the sea – as occasionally happens – even when, for a considerable length of time, the submarine could not previously have been visible from the enemy ship.

112.) The overhauling maneuver requires a high degree of tactical ability; its success is the pre-condition of the following underwater attack, and therefore the success of the operation. As a tactical masterpiece, the overhauling maneuver is therefore the exclusive business of the commander, and its preparation and execution require his unremitting attention.

113.) In fighting its way forward to the position ahead of the beam of the enemy, in borderline conditions of visibility during the day, the submarine is engaged in a long, drawn-out and extremely tiring overhauling operation. It is an incessant "nibbling at the horizon" going in again and again as soon as the tops of the masts get smaller, and sheering off again at once, as soon as they rise higher again. These strenuous efforts to overhaul the enemy are continued, in the Atlantic, hour by hour, and can only succeed as a result of indomitable resolution and an unchanging, obstinate refusal to let the enemy escape, even when the submarine finds that progress is very slow. Any change of course on the part of the enemy, or engine trouble, etc., occurring on board the enemy ship, may immediately alter the position in favor of the submarine.

114.) The overhauling maneuver should always be exploited, in order to obtain the particulars of the enemy (course, speed, pattern of the zigzag course) by careful observation of the course of the submarine itself, exact D/F of the enemy ship, estimation of range and position at regular intervals of time. These particulars are almost always more reliable than those obtained underwater.

115.) The overhauling maneuver and the attack should not be abandoned even when the bearing shows little movement of the enemy. Do not let the difficulties wear you down!

[. . .]

117.) Whether or not – in view of the low surface and underwater speed of the submarine – an overhauling maneuver in daylight is bound to succeed depends on the speed of the enemy and his position when sighted. If the enemy escort is well forward of the ships, or if the enemy has an air escort, so that the submarine is forced to dive both frequently and prematurely, thus further reducing its already low speed, the overhauling maneuver meets with an additional serious difficulty. But in this one case also, the submarine commander must show determination, and not yield anything unnecessarily.

118.) If the submarine is temporarily forced under the surface by the enemy escort, etc., it must not stay down too long. It should always try to surface again as soon as possible, in order to observe the enemy better and not to lose valuable time without a good reason.

119.) In case of sudden deterioration of visibility, due to squalls of rain, etc.; caution should be observed. The submarine should submerge again, if improving visibility reveals that it has approached too near to the enemy while unable to see him.

120.) When the submarine has reached the necessary position forward of the enemy's beam, that is to say, the counter D/F position in relation, to the general course ascertained for the enemy (see No. 108), it must move toward the enemy on the surface and underwater, always in the endeavor to get in a shot (discharge a torpedo) as soon as possible, before the position changes, i.e., before, for example, the enemy changes course, in such a way as to foil the attack.

[. . .]

The view of a hostile merchant ship through the periscope of a British submarine.

C. Carrying Out the Underwater Attack.

125.) The "sparing" use of the periscope; i.e., the raising of the periscope, at frequent intervals and for a brief space of time, to surface level, so that the periscope appears no bigger than a fist, and almost constantly awash, begins at a distance of approximately 4,000–5,000 m from the enemy, according to the state of the weather and the conditions of light. It is a mistake to keep the periscope down for any length time when the enemy is near. In that case the submarine is not less visible during the "sparing" use of the periscope; but it can itself see nothing, and is therefore in greater danger. Consequently, the submarine should carry out frequent observations of short duration; but, in all circumstances, they should be repeated again and again.

126.) The periscope should only be raised when the submarine is traveling at low speed. Before raising the periscope, it is therefore necessary to reduce the speed. Otherwise, if the sea is calm, the wake of the periscope can easily be seen, besides which the periscope of a submarine traveling at speed will cause splashes, and a conspicuous feather [*Wasserfahne*].

127.) If special reasons require that the speed be temporarily increased, for example, in order to reach a position more suitable for launching an attack, the periscope must be lowered until the top of it is at least 1 m under the surface. When the submarine is at the depth for attack, the periscope should not, however, be further lowered to an extent greater than it is absolutely necessary, in order not unnecessarily to lose time in raising it again.

128.) In a calm sea, the screw of the submarine causes a slight ripple which is visible on the surface. If it is necessary in this case to proceed at speed, the periscope should therefore be taken down altogether, and the submarine should dive to 18 m, insofar as the position (nearness) of the enemy will allow this.

129.) Towards the end of the attack, just before the torpedo is launched, it must suffice for the torpedo aimer ("T.C.O."), on completing the computation of the enemy's course and position, to see only the tops of the funnels and masts of the enemy.

130.) For computing the range, the 1 magnification should be used in the periscope. With the 6-fold magnification, no estimation of distance is possible, on account of the monocular optical system of the periscope.

As a matter of principles the 6-fold magnification of the periscope should always only be used temporarily, in order the better to observe details of the enemy ship, as, for example, in computing its course and speed, but never for the actual attack at close range.

131.) At a distance of about 4,000 to 2,000 m, according to the speed and position of the enemy, the submarine begins to go in for the attack.

The following rule of thumb serves to determine, in good time, the distance of the submarine When about launch the attack, (torpedo) abreast of the enemy.

In position 5°, the lateral distance from the enemy = 1/10, in position 10° = 1/5, in position 15° = 1/4, in position 20° = 1/3, in position 30° = 1/2 of the momentary distance.

132.) The danger of being located by sound location during the attack at close range must be countered, as far as circumstances allow, by traveling at as slow a speed as possible, and by absolute silence on board the submarine.

133.) The underwater attack is also practicable at dawn and dusk, and on moonlit nights. In these cases, the following points should be observed:

a) Complete blacking out of the conning tower and the control room is necessary, as otherwise the light is still reflected, to a considerable extent, in the periscope.

b) The estimation of distances and positions at night by means of the periscope meets with great difficulties. The submarine may easily be nearer to the enemy than is supposed.

c) At night, all periscope operations should be undertaken with the 1 magnification, on account of the improved effect of the optical system when using small magnifications.

d) The observation of the enemy against whom the attack is directed, and the all-round view in respect of the position in relation to other nearby vessels, can then be undertaken, in certain circumstances, by two periscopes.

134.) The rare opportunity of attacking an enemy concentration of ships must be used, by going all out, with all the torpedoes, even in spite of the strongest enemy escort. One of the ships of the concentration should be attacked, and the attack carried out, by a method suited to the position of the target, in a manner calculated to annihilate the latter; immediately afterwards a second and third ships should be attacked where possible.

135.) The shape of a concentration of ships is difficult to make out from periscope depth, and at a distance. If the enemy group is a broad one (blunt formation, line abreast, double line ahead, broken formation) it is advantageous to let one's self run into the formation from the front, and to fire torpedoes from an angle. The advantages of this position in the enemy group are: less efficient covering and less vigilance on the part of the enemy, and consequently maximum deliberation in carrying out the attack.

In attacking a pointed formation, the open side is more favorable, because the chances of a hit are better (the targets overlap). In addition, on the open side the submarine is in less danger of being rammed, and can therefore carry out the attack with more deliberation.

136.) If, during an attack on a convoy, the necessity arises of diving suddenly to a depth of 20 m, as a protection against escorting ships or air attack (i.e., because there is a danger of being rammed or spotted) the attack must on no account be finally abandoned because of that necessity. In view of the fact that, when traveling at the depth of 20 m, the submarine loses count of the position in the direction of the attack, it may then in certain circumstances be advisable to turn away from the convoy, at full speed, and turn down again with little divergence from the general course of the enemy, in order to resume the attack from the outside. If the convoy is a long one, there is then always a chance of getting in a shot at the last ships.

[. . .]

D. Methods of Attack; Underwater Discharging of Torpedoes.

141.) The ordinary underwater attack is carried out with the aid of the fire control system, at maximum range. If the entire fire control system fails to function, and in the case of unexplained misses, the bow torpedo attack proper is called for. These methods of attack must also be mastered by the submarine commander, and used according to circumstances.

I. Maximum Range Attack.

142.) Advantages of the maximum range attack.

a) The commander is free from the necessity of calculating the direction of the attack, and of maneuvering on this course, and can devote his attention entirely to securing a favorable position for the attack. The only necessity is to get the target into the angle covered by the torpedoes with the minimum firing range.

b) The possibilities of using the torpedo are considerably greater, as in case of necessity, the entire angle range of the torpedo can always be exploited, and the torpedo discharged in any direction.

c) The fire control system takes into account the parallax in the torpedo tube, so that, if the firing data are correct, the marking point usually coincides with the center of the target.

d) The range can always be read off, and the angle of dispersion [transfer] and the turning circle of the submarine can quickly be embodied in the calculation for improving the aiming angle, and used through the medium of the fire control system.

e) Difficult and quickly changing situations (high speed of the enemy, frequent changes of course) can be mastered by a submarine with fire control in circumstances in which a submarine without fire control is forced to renounce the torpedo attack because of the inability of the submarine to turn quickly under water.

143.) The important difficulty of the maximum range torpedo attack – and this also applies to every angle attack – is the accurate computation of the distance as a basis for the improvement of the convergence. In case of uncertainty in assessing the distance, more especially in firing at close range, and during engagements *en passant*, one should therefore always endeavor to fire at as small an angle as possible, in order to avoid missing as a result of false convergence values. If the angle is large, a false calculation of distance, especially of distances under 1,000 m, results in materially wrong measurements on the target, due to the error of convergence.

144.) In view of the fact that the maximum range attack, when carried out underwater, unlike the bow attack proper, requires complicated technical equipment with a comparatively large personnel, so that the number of possible sources of error is correspondingly greater, careful training of all the operators, and close attention to the equipment, are a special necessity.

145.) If the electric system of the fire control is out of action do not at once fall back on the primitive methods of the bow, stern or angle attack, but use to the full the reserve possibilities of the plant (predictor as a mechanical firing angle computer). There should be frequent rehearsals of the procedure to be applied when the electric system of the fire control is out of action.

II. Bow Torpedo Attack Proper.

146.) Procedure:

a) Determine the enemy's course by position and bearing;

b) Compute the enemy's speed;

c) Ascertain the director angle for the required firing position;

d) put the submarine on the course for the attack;

the course for the attack = cross D/F of the enemy + (starboard) - (port) director angle, according to whether the starboard or the port of the enemy is to be attacked,

If it is intended to attack from a narrower angle, the bearing in the position to be taken up when discharging the torpedo should be set for calculating the course for the attack, instead of the diagonal bearing of the target.

e) By "flanking" the course (i.e., keeping ahead of, or behind, the direction of the attack), the submarine should approach to within close range, and take up a favorable position (near position 90° etc.). In doing is, constant observation of the growth of the enemy's bearing and constantly repeated computations of the distance, while using the periscope sparingly, are a necessity.

f) If the enemy's course has been correctly ascertained, and his speed correctly assessed, the enemy must be in position 90° etc. when he enters the D 3 A. If this does not happen, the moment of firing must be anticipated or retarded, by discharging the torpedo while turning toward, or away from, the target, in order to exploit a more favorable enemy position.

III. The Stern Torpedo Attack Proper.

147.) The stern torpedo attack proper can only be carried out either when the position of the submarine is to the right, ahead of the enemy, or when, in consequence of a sudden change of course on the part of the enemy, the use of the stern torpedo tube is more advantageous than the use of the bow torpedo tubes. Procedure:

a) If the submarine is ahead of the enemy, it must go to meet him, in order to carry out the stern torpedo attack. Moving toward the enemy is better than moving with him, because, in this case, the submarine, in turning away to take up the direction of attack, has less turning to do to the extent of the double the D.A. [director angle].

b) Ascertain the course and speed of the enemy.

c) Determine the director angle for the required firing position = 90° etc.

d) Set the submarine on the course for the attack. The change of course should be effected according to the speed at which the enemy is approaching. Do not turn too quickly, as otherwise the range becomes too long. Keep your head.

Direction of attack = Counter D/F to cross D/F + (starboard) director angle, - (port)

according to whether the starboard or the port side is being attacked. If the attack is to take place from a narrower angle, the counter D/F of the D/F in each position envisaged for the discharging of the torpedo, for example 60°, should be set instead of the counter D/F of the cross D/F of the enemy.

IV. Angled Attack. [Gyro Angling]

148.) The angled attack has the following important advantages:

a) The submarine is able to move more freely in carrying out the attack, and need not, as it has to do when making a bow attack proper, approach the enemy almost "end on," keeping the enemy's position, and the distance, under constant observation.

b) The submarine does not cross the courses of the enemy's escorting ships to the same extent as when carrying out the bow torpedo attack proper.

c) In case of a too-closely developed bow attack, or of sudden changes of course on the part of the enemy, it is still possible to fire a torpedo.

d) If the enemy formation is a broad one, the angled attack affords the best opportunity of attacking several targets on either side, by allowing one's self to be overtaken by the formation.

149.) The angled attack consists mainly of:

1. The 45° angled shot.
2. The 90° angled shot.

The commander can make use of other methods of angled attack, if 14 is. able to make the necessary calculations during the attack, without their having been especially rehearsed, as have the two most usual methods of angled attack.

1. The 45° angled shot.
150.) Method of carrying out the attack:
    a) Set the submarine on the, course
          aa) Bows 45°, angle shot;
Running Fight (Bows of the submarine in the same direction as the course of the enemy)

Direction of attack (course) = Diagonal D/F of the enemy + (starboard)
                                     - (port)
(45° + director angle), according to whether the starboard or the port side of the target is to be attacked.

When firing from a narrower position, the procedure as in the bow torpedo attack proper, is to set the D/F in the position for launching the torpedo, for the purpose of calculating the direction of attack, for example 60° instead of the diagonal D/F of the target.

    Engagement *en passant* (bows of the submarine in the opposite direction to the course of the enemy):

Direction of Attack (course) = Diagonal D/F of the enemy - (starboard)
                                     + (port)
(45° - director angle), according to whether the starboard or the port side of the target is being attacked.

    bb) 45° stern angled shot:
    a) Running fight (bows of the submarine in the same direction as the course of the enemy):
        Direction of Attack = Counter D/F to diagonal D/F of the enemy
                      + (port) (45° = director angle), - (starboard)

according to whether the starboard or the port side is attacked. For narrower positions, the procedure in calculating the course (direction of the attack) is the same as has been described in dealing with the other methods of attack, previously mentioned.

    Engagement *en passant* (bows of the submarine in the opposite direction to the course of the enemy):

Direction of Attack (course) = Counter D/F to diagonal D/F of the enemy
+ (starboard) (45° = director angle) - (port)

according to whether the starboard or the port side is attacked.

b) Set the director angle. Turn the graduated dial on the rim of the periscope by 45° away from the 0° mark toward the target, and then adjust the director angle from the 45° mark to the position of the target; i.e., if the enemy course is to the left, the director angle must be set to the left of the 45° mark, and vice versa. Points to be observed: The director angle always lies *outside* the 45° torpedo angle, when the torpedo, before it turns, travels in the same direction as the target (for the bow angle attack in running fights, for the stern angle attack in engagements *en passant*; the director angle lies *inside* the 45° torpedo angle, when the torpedo, before turning, travels in the opposite direction to the target (for the bow angle attack in engagement en passant, for the stern angle attack in running fights). In both cases, however, the director angle should always be set in the direction of the target from the 45° mark.

c) For convergence 50, allow for forward or backward movement; for the former, when the torpedo, before turning, moves in the opposite direction to the target (for the bow angle attack in engagements en passant, for the stern angle attack in running fights), and for the latter, when the torpedo, before turning, moves in the same direction as the target (for the bow angle attack in running fights, for the stern angle attack in engagements *en passant*).

2. The 90° angled shot.

151.) The 90° angled attack should only be used for small convergences; i.e., when the torpedo, before turning, moves in the same direction as the target. It is very difficult to estimate the D.A. for large convergences, especially in attacking at short range.

Consequently, the 90° angled shot with a small convergent displacement of the target is used: in running fights in the form of the bow torpedo attack; in engagements *en passant* in the form of the stern torpedo attack.

152.) Procedure.

a) Set the submarine on the direction of attack (course). aa) 90° bow angled shot in running fights:

Direction of attack (course) = Counter D/F of diagonal D/F - (starboard)
+ (port)

(90° + director angle), according to whether the starboard or port side of the target is being attacked.

The crew of a U-boat at sea grab the opportunity for a brief meal in a tiny galley area.

When attacking from a narrower position, the direction of attack (course) is calculated in the same way as in the methods of attack previously indicated; i.e., instead of the diagonal D/F of the target, the D/F in the position for launching the torpedo, for example 60°, or the counter D/F of the bearing, is used for the calculation. bb) 90° stern angled shot in engagements en passant

Direction of attack (course) = Diagonal D/F of the target - (starboard) + (port) (90° - director angle), according to whether the starboard or port side of the target is attacked.

b) Set the director angle. Turn the graduated dial on the rim of the periscope by 90° away from the 0° mark towards the target, and then adjust the director angle from the 90° mark to the position of the target; i.e., if the enemy course is to the left, the director angle must be set to the left of the 90° mark, and vice versa (see also No. 146, b).

c) For the convergence allow room for backward movement.

153.) The chief difficulty of the maximum range torpedo attack – and this also applies to every angled attack – is the precise calculation of the distance as a basis for the improvement of the convergence. In case of uncertainty in estimating the distance (range), more especially in launching torpedoes at close range, and during engagements *en passant*, the object to be achieved is always to fire at the minimum angle, in order to avoid misses resulting from false convergence values. If the angle is large, a false estimation of distance, especially of distances under 1,000 m, results in materially wrong measurements on the target, due to the error of convergence.

[. . .]

Section V
The Submarine as a Gunnery Vessel.

271.) The submarine as a gunnery vessel is in itself properly a contradiction in terms. Being incapable of offering powerful resistance, and because of its low and unstable gunnery and controlling platforms, which are directly exposed to the action of the sea, it cannot be said to be built for artillery combat. In the use of gunnery, the submarine proper is fundamentally inferior to any surface vessel of war, because every gunnery duel means that for the submarine, unlike its adversary on the surface, everything is at stake, since a hit on the body of the submarine may render it incapable of diving, and thus lead to its total loss.

A gunnery duel between the submarine proper, i.e., the torpedo-carrying submarine as a weapon of attack, and surface vessels of war, is therefore impracticable.

272.) For the torpedo-firing submarine, the gunnery is and remains a minor weapon, to be used on occasion, because the use of gunnery – openly and on the surface – runs counter to the primary purpose of the submarine, which is the surprise underwater attack.

In accordance with this fundamental fact, the torpedo-firing submarine uses only its gunnery in waging war against merchant shipping, that is to say, for the purpose of stopping steamers, or of overcoming the resistance of unarmed or weakly armed vessels.

273.) Every time the commander resorts to the use of gunnery, he must bear in mind that, in wartime, almost all enemy merchant ships are armed, and that neutral markings are no proof that the ships thus marked really are neutral, and harmless.

274.) The use of gunnery against an armed enemy can only succeed if heavy hits are at once scored on the enemy, at minimum range with the help of the element of surprise, and if the submarine is also in a position to prevent the manning and use of the enemy's gunnery, by bringing all its light weapons to bear on the enemy.

275.)

a) This achieved by the "gunnery-raid"– at dusk, or after dark, with all weapons at minimum range (6 to 11 hm) [hm = hectometre; 1 hm = 100m]. During the day, or on light moonlit nights, a gunnery attack at long range can only succeed if the enemy is poorly armed, or unarmed.

b) The preliminary conditions for the success of a gunnery raid are: adequate special training (including night training); careful planning and careful material preparation of the attack; individual training in the use of the individual weapons.

c) Procedure:

1.) Gun commander and crew take up action stations in good time on the conning tower and the upper deck, in order to get used to the darkness. Precise arrangements are to be made regarding method of covering the target. 10.5 cm are to be fired at the bridge and superstructures, beginning with 10 rounds of incendiary shells, in order to get a good marking point in the resulting fire. 3.7 cm machine gun m34 to be fired at the stern (gun). 2 cm (powerful dazzling effect) should only be fired on orders of the commander, when there is a jam (stoppage) in the 3.7 cm gun.

2.) After the type and armament of the enemy ship have been ascertained (in case of necessity, by underwater observation during the day):

aa) Approach the steamer cautiously from the rear, by stages making use of the conditions of light, sea and wind. Open fire as soon as the submarine is level with the steamer. Range according to darkness, in no circumstances more than 6 to 8 hm.;

bb) or overhaul on the boundary of the zone of visibility to position 50 to 60. Approach on the "dog course," slowly or at full speed, to reach range 800 and position approximately 100. Rudder hard over by 6 to 7 "DEZ" to the direction of the running fight, with a slight shortening of the range. Open fire as soon as you are on the course. This method has the advantage of a quicker passage through the danger zone, and, on the other hand, the disadvantage of attacking from a sector which can be better observed by the enemy;

cc) or overhaul on the boundary of the zone of visibility until the narrow position is reached, approach on the "dog course," and maneuver in such a way that the range in position 90 is about 5 to 8 hm; then open up with your guns like a bolt out of the blue, at the same time increasing the speed of the submarine. The submarine, firing its guns, passes behind the stern of the enemy ship, and is in a position at any moment to shorten or keep the range, by turning in toward the enemy, or following the course to engage in a running fight, or, if the enemy puts up a strong defence, to bring about a rapid increase of range by turning away and accelerating its speed.

dd) It is not advisable to fight an engagement *en passant* at the guns fire crosswise, and it is difficult to keep the reckoning, owing to the movement (change of bearing) of the target.

3.) The second shot must hit the mark. Bridge and superstructures are big targets, and soon burn. (It is particularly important that the ship should burn, as the gun commanders are dazzled by the flames, and marking is rendered very difficult.) According to circumstances, concentrate the gunfire on one part of the ship. At close range, machine guns m34 are very effective in suppressing enemy resistance.

If, after the first artillery attack, enemy fire is still to be reckoned with, it is advisable to attack with short bursts (approximately 6 to 8 rounds 10.5 cm or 8.8 cm, and, proportionately, 3.7 cm or 2 cm), and beat down the enemy resistance without exposing the submarine by staying too long near the enemy.

In order to sink the ship quicker the fire should afterwards be directed only at the bows or the stern. On an even keel, ships only sink slowly.

Firing from a position ahead of the beam should be avoided, on account of the blinding effect of the flash.

d) In carrying out the artillery raid, a sharp lookout should be kept (first officer of the watch) to leeward of the gunfire. In certain circumstances, it is advisable, as soon as a certain effect of the bombardment is noticed on the enemy ship (collapse of the defence), to interrupt the attack, and to take up a position on the other side of the enemy, in order to watch the sea on that side.

276.) As soon as the enemy ship, in an artillery duel, begins to find the range, the submarine must turn away or submerge.

277.) In areas not frequently patrolled by the enemy, the use of artillery against ships which have been hit by a torpedo, but are still afloat, is likely to be successful, and saves torpedoes. The attack on ships whose engines have been put out of action should be carried out from a position ahead or astern, according to the disposition of the guns.

278.) Hints concerning the use of gunnery.

a) Before the submarine surfaces for the artillery attack, the gun crew must assemble in the control room ready for action, with all equipment (ammunition cases open, ammunition feed prepared), so as to get the gun ready to fire in the shortest possible time after surfacing.

b) In carrying out a gunnery attack after surfacing, the order "ready to fire" must not be given until the commander has satisfied himself from the conning tower that the general position, as well as the navigational conditions (submarine sufficiently out of the water) are favorable.

c) As a matter of principle, the entire gun crew, including those in charge of the magazine, should always be strapped on while working. The danger of falling overboard is great and the fishing for men who have fallen to water costs valuable time.

d) Ammunition is to be protected from being wet by splashes (spray). Wet ammunition causes the bursting of cartridge cases, and thereby in certain circumstances troublesome stoppages.

e) During every gunnery engagement, a constant sharp watch should be kept (air and horizon). Carelessness of the watch is dangerous.
[. . .]

Section VII
Submarine Warfare on Merchant Shipping.

A. General.
290.) In the struggle against the enemy sea communications, i.e., in the destruction of the enemy's overseas trade, the submarine is a particularly suitable naval weapon with which to challenge the enemy's naval superiority. The continuous successful use of the submarine in the war on merchant shipping is, therefore, in the long run, of decisive strategical importance for the total course of the war, since the enemy, who is dependent on his overseas trade, is in the position that, for him, the loss of his sea communications means the loss of the war.

291.) The suitability of the submarine for use in the war on merchant shipping depends, again, on its eminent advantage of invisibility. The submarine is thus in a position to carry on the war against the enemy's communications in all sea areas, including areas of undisputed enemy domination.
[. . .]

293.) The enemy seeks to counter the danger of submarine operations on the routes of solitary ships, by arming the ships, in order to prevent the successful use of the submarine's gunnery, and to compel the submarine to use the more expensive torpedo, thus reducing its chances of success and its effective stay in the theater of operations.

294.) Another defensive measure of the enemy against the use of the submarine in the war on merchant shipping is the formation of convoys under the protection of war-ships. As a result of the concentration of numerous steamers to form convoys, the sea routes lose their characteristic peacetime appearance and become desolate, as it is only at relatively long intervals that a concentration of steamers passes along them.

To achieve decisive successes against such concentrations of steamers, a concentration of submarines is necessary, because the lone submarine can only achieve partial success against a convoy.

295.) The general rule for the use and the offensive operations of the submarine in the war against merchant shipping is to station the submarines, whenever possible, at points where the traffic is thickest. In doing this, the submarines should be free and mobile in their operations, while in narrow coastal waters, on the other hand, their positions should be stationary.

296.) If a sufficient number of submarines is available, they must assemble on the enemy sea routes at a sufficient depth, but also in sufficient breadth, to be able to contact enemy sea traffic, which, in wartime, will avoid the usual peace routes, make long detours, and come from many different directions.

297.) Within range of our own air bases, where air reconnaissance of the enemy sea communications is practicable, extensive mutual support by the air arm and the submarines in the common war against enemy overseas trade will be possible.

[. . .]

C. How to deal with Convoys.

310.) The most important task within which the submarine is faced on sighting enemy convoys is to attack them, and to endeavor to repeat the attack again and again. The submarine must not allow itself to be shaken off. If it is temporarily repulsed or forced to submerge, it must continue to press on, again and again, in the direction of the general course of the convoy, seek to contact it, and renew the attack.

311.) In keeping contact with convoys, and carrying out the attacks, no attention should be paid to consumption of fuel, provided that enough fuel is saved to enable the submarine to return to its base.

312.)

a) On sighting convoys and other important objectives, in order that these may be attacked by other submarines as well, the submarine should report the sighting immediately, even before attacking itself, and send further reports confirming the contact, in the intervals between its attacks on the enemy ships.

b) Failing orders to the contrary, the most important thing always is to attack. Each submarine should be concerned primarily with carrying out its own attack. Exceptions, for example, for boats whose task it is to maintain the contact with the convoy, must be in accordance with orders from Headquarters.

c) For the information of other boats, the intention to attack should be communicated by short signals according to the "Short Signal Book," pages. 1, 4 and 83.

The possible disadvantage of warning the enemy by these wireless messages is bound to be less serious than when, as a result of the omission of the messages, other submarines fail to contact the targets at all.

313.) The success, or otherwise, of the attacks of all the other submarines operating against the convoy depends on the skill of the first submarine, whose duty it is to keep the contact with the convoy.

314.)

a) The essential contents of the reports must always be: Position, course, and speed on the enemy. Type, strength, and distribution of the enemy covering forces, and the state of the weather should be reported later to supplement these messages. Attention should be paid to the conditions of visibility and the resulting possibilities of error in estimating the distance for the reports on the position of the enemy.

b) Try to ascertain the general course of the enemy as soon as possible, from the reckoning, and report it as such.

315.) While carrying out its own attack, the submarine must transmit regular and complete contact reports, according to the following headings:

a) The two first boats to make contact, acting as "contact holders," transmit complete hourly reports.

b) As long as the two first boats transmit contact reports, the other boats signal "made contact!" once only, as soon as they have reached the convoy, or, analogously, "lost contact!", using short signals in both cases.

c) If a "contact holder" fails to send reports for longer than 1 hours, another boat must take over. This must be done without waiting for orders.

d) If a "contact holder" loses contact, it must report as soon as possible the last position of the enemy, and his course and speed.

A U-boat commander on the bridge of his submarine keeps a close watch over an Allied convoy, planning the best route of attack and escape.

e) All boats which have been in contact with the convoy, and lost ground in consequence of their long stay underwater, or have been driven off, must also report their own position.

316.) The "contact holders" also operate as is best for the purposes of their attack. Do not endanger your own overhauling maneuver, and the success of the attack, by approaching too close, in order to obtain (more) accurate firing data.

317.) The arrangements for guiding further submarines to the spot are greatly facilitated by the emission of D/F signals by the submarine maintaining the contact. At intervals of half an hour, the "contact holder" sends out D/F signals and a wireless signal, on a long wave-length fixed by Headquarters, defining the D/F and the distance from the enemy, according to "Standing War Orders for Submarine Commanders" ("St.Kriegsbor.B.d.U."), either at the request of other submarines, or on orders of the "Home Submarine

Command," or, in certain circumstances, on its own initiative, if such orders are not received in time, and there is reason to believe that there are other submarines about. If the commander decides to send out D/F signals on his own initiative, the other submarines should first be notified by means of a wireless message or signal on the submarine's short wave.

318.) The transmission of D/F signals, however, always creates an additional danger that the "contact holder" will be spotted; consequently:

a) Do not ask for D/F signals if dead reckoning and visibility are good.

b) Ask for D/F signals if the dead reckoning is wrong, visibility is very bad, or if nothing is sighted on the computed point of contact.

319.) The following are the rules for keeping the contact, and overhauling:

a) Overhaul right on the limits of the zone of visibility. Be absolutely sure that you are not sighted.

b) Keep the contact by the mast-tops or the smoke from the funnels. The smoke is quite sufficient. If it disappears temporarily, it does not mean that you have lost contact. Go forward only after nothing has been seen for a certain length of time, and regain contact.

c) Keep the sharpest possible lookout, so as to see the masts, and to be able to tell when they increase in height, and then to make off at full speed. At the same time, endeavor to lose no ground, but to get to the fore. If the distance from the enemy continues to be insufficient, submerge – go down to periscope depth. As soon as the position is clear, surface again.

d) If your position is behind the convoy, do not allow yourself to be driven too far back by the rear covering forces, but submerge in good time. In this way, you avoid, to a great extent, loss of ground, and gain time for a continuance of the pursuit.

e) Keep the sharpest possible lookout in the direction away from the enemy. In this direction, surprises may easily occur as a result of the enemy's sending out escorting vessels to a considerable distance, on the flanks and astern of the convoy, or as a result of the arrival of long-distance escorting units. Behavior of the submarine is according to c).

320.) Apart from the clever tactics on the part of the submarine engaged in maintaining the contact with, and overhauling, the convoy, a decisive factor in the use of other submarines is faultless navigation on the part of both the "contact holder" and all the other boats. In the theater of operations, it is therefore the imperative duty of the commander to seize on all possibilities for the purpose of ensuring efficient navigation. This necessitates, whenever possible, repeated reckonings during the day. A feeling for loss of speed and drift owing to the motion of the sea should be cultivated.

If errors of reckoning are discovered, the contact reports should be rectified at once, and attention called to the previous error; this should also be done, in case of necessity, by other submarines which detect false reckonings in the reports of the "contact holder" proper.

[. . .]

322.) The object of every overhauling maneuver is to attack as soon as possible; this important object should not be jeopardized by carelessness. Consequently, it is better to stay further out in the overhauling maneuver than to go too close in, and run the risk of being spotted and forced to submerge, thus losing leeway for the attack, and time.

323.) It is only in case of inescapable necessity that the attack should be put off, for example, at dusk – if it is already too dark for the underwater launching of torpedoes – with the object of carrying out a surface attack with more certainty of success after darkness has fallen; or at dawn – if it is already too light for a sure aim at close quarters on the surface – with the object of carrying out a safe underwater attack at short range as soon as it gets light enough for that purpose.

324.) If the enemy's air and sea escort is so strong that it is not possible to overhaul in daytime, the attack should be postponed until nightfall. Nevertheless, for this purpose, the submarine should overhaul in good time during the day. At the least, it should be level with the convoy when twilight comes. The overhauling maneuver should not be put off till evening. There is a danger of being compelled to submerge, or of having to retreat to a distance, in consequence of the enemy's reconnaissance patrols, thus losing contact with the convoy.

325.) If the submarine is temporarily compelled to submerge by the escorting forces of the enemy, it should not remain down too long. Surface again as soon as the position allows, in order to advance more quickly, and take up a position for the attack, and also in order to observe better, and to be able to transmit contact reports.

326.) It is possible to keep the contact with the convoy in spite of the enemy's covering forces, or his air escort. The conditions for attack are, indeed, rendered more difficult by the presence of a strong escort, and by air cover, and more time is needed to mount the attack, but it is still possible, if the submarine commander acts with steadfastness and determination, to keep the contact. If the attack can no longer be successfully carried out by day, the submarine must get in a torpedo at night.

a) In the neighborhood of the convoy, no submarine must be deterred from carrying out an attack by the fact that the enemy ASDIC operations have been observed. The distance of an adversary engaged in ASDIC hunting cannot be ascertained; the wireless D/F computer receives the enemy D/F at a greater distance than the latter can cover in target finding. For example, the enemy, while carrying out his D/F operations, may occupy a position well beyond the dip of the horizon, and have not located the submarine at all. Always remember, therefore, that the enemy can only attack what he sees, and that the submarine is more difficult to make out than he is himself. Consequently, the submarine commander should rely on himself and his lookout, and not become the slave of an instrument.

327.) If, for any reason, the submarine has failed to contact the enemy during the night, that is not a reason for giving up the attack. The submarine should keep obstinately on the track of the enemy. The chase may go on for days before the first success is achieved against a convoy.

328.) In keeping the contact, the greatest care should be exercised during the transition from day to night, especially in the Atlantic, in southern latitudes. Here the twilight is so short that the transition from day to night comes with the utmost suddenness. At nightfall, the submarine maintaining the contact is therefore still at a distance almost equal to the appropriate distance by day and must go close in at once, resolutely and at top speed.

The possibility must always be reckoned with that the enemy will go well out and double after dark, effecting, apart from the zigzag movements as far observed, an important change of course, in order to shake off any pursuing submarines. In addition, at sunset (and perhaps during the day, if visibility becomes poor), the enemy will usually send out fast vessels of the escort, which search the sea in the rear of the convoy with the object of forcing any pursuing submarines underwater until the convoy is out of sight, and has carried out, unnoticed, the usual evening change of course. These escort vessels sent out to reconnoiter, and shake off submarine "contact holders," always return to the convoy, feigning to take a different course.

329.) When engaged in operations against convoys, based on contact reports, the meeting point with the convoy should always be fixed sufficiently far ahead of it, according to the conditions of visibility, for example 10 to 14 sm.

330.) If a submarine, on receipt of contact reports, is a good distance ahead of the convoy, it must exercise care in going to meet it, as otherwise it may easily lose ground by advancing too far.

331.) Troublesome sweepers of the enemy escort must be destroyed, if an opportunity offers to attack them. The destruction of covering ships, above all, of cruiser escorts, destroyers, etc., is in the interests of all the submarines which are already in contact with the convoy, or are to be used to attack it.

332.)

a) Submarine traps must also be reckoned with in dealing with convoys. These have instructions to station themselves among the last steamers, and to fall behind, pretending that they have engine trouble, etc., in order thus to attract attacking submarines, to lead them away from the convoy, and to be able to attack them. Be cautious, therefore, when attacking steamers sailing behind convoys.

b) It has been observed that groups of escort ships, emitting clouds of smoke, frequently collect behind convoys for the purpose of deceiving the submarines, and drawing them away from the convoy. The commander must not be led astray by these tactics. In case he is not certain that he is in contact with the convoy, he should make up his contact report accordingly: for example, "big clouds of smoke" or "ships belching smoke."

333.) If several boats are being used in the attack, none of them must break off the pursuit merely because it has used up its torpedoes. It must follow the convoy, seeking to contact it, and maintain the contact. As there is no longer a target, it should take up the most favorable position as a "contact holder" (for example, sun, convoy and submarine in time), and continue to send messages. The boat will be ordered back as soon as possible.

334.) When contact has been lost, a systematic search must be made by the submarines. The commander must first form a clear idea of the position, on the basis of his own observations and the reports of the other boats. After that, the submarine should carry out reconnaissance patrols at top speed. In poor visibility, and at night, submerge frequently, and listen (sound-location). Do not give up if D/F sound location at first fails to produce results. Submerge again, and follow up.

335.) If other boats are encountered during the pursuit of a convoy, go in signaling range or earshot. Compare notes. Arrange reconnaissance.

336.) Conjectures and positive indications as to the position of the convoy (for example, sightings of aircraft, track of steamers, solitary ships, results of sound location, detonations, star shells), and the courses of unsuccessful reconnaissance patrols, should be reported by W.T. Report all particulars likely to be of use in clarifying the position, more especially when it emerges from an order to attack that the impression of the position at headquarters is erroneous. A clear conception of the tactical possibilities of the situation is a pre-condition for the transmission of correct reports.

337.) As soon as the impression is created that contact can only be made by means of a guided attack, and not by submarines acting on their own initiative, orders are issued prescribing certain groupings, there is the method of directional reconnaissance, and reconnaissance in sectors.

338.) In the directional reconnaissance method, each submarine is allotted a certain strip of the area to be searched, in which it must carry out a systematic search at high speed, on a zigzag course, for an enemy presumed to pass through a certain limited zone. The number and angle of the zigzags, and consequently the thoroughness of the search, depends on weather and visibility, and the speed margin of the submarine.

339.) When the area to be searched is divided, for the above purpose, into sectors, one sector is dealt with by each submarine, the apex of the sector being the last known position of the convoy. If at all possible, the search should be commenced at the apex of the sector. The sector should be covered by the submarine in both zigzags and in "strips," until the whole area has been searched up to the highest limits of the reported course of the enemy, then it should carry the search to the boundaries of the sector for the high rates of speed. As soon as the upper limit is reached, remain there until the convoy must be assumed to have passed through the sector at low rates of speed; or begin the inward search.

a) The submarines may only abandon an operation which they have been ordered to carry out when the necessity to do so is inescapable. In such cases the abandonment of the operation must be reported immediately.

If a submarine is of the opinion that it is inadvisable to continue an operation assigned to it by the command, for special reasons that are unknown to the latter, it must mention the reasons and ask for fresh orders.

b) The replacement of torpedoes while the submarine is keeping the contact must not result in the loss of the contact; consequently:

1.) If at all possible, reloading should be effected above water, while maintaining the contact. At the same time, care should be taken that the submarine is always ready to submerge.

2.) If the state of the weather compels the submarine to dive for the purpose of reloading, then only as many torpedoes should be loaded at once as will not interrupt the contact with the convoy. For example: first submerge, then reload a torpedo, then surface, then follow the convoy, and then, after catching up with it, load again.

3.) If an improvement in the weather is in sight, wait to recharge until this is possible on the surface, in case there is then still a chance to attack.

4.) All preparations for reloading torpedoes are to be made before submerging!

Section VIII
Operating in Packs; Reconnaissance and Attack.

A. General.

340.) The object of the common attack is to produce contact between a number of submarines and an adversary who has been located by a submarine or another reconnaissance unit, to maintain that contact, and to destroy the enemy.

This object is attained by holding on obstinately to the enemy, and by the transmission of unambiguous messages by the "contact holder," as well as by immediate action of the other submarines, *on their own initiative*, after receipt of the first contact report. A special order calling for such independent action is only required in exceptional circumstances.

The pre-condition of success is – in addition to an aggressive spirit, a capacity for making quick decisions, initiative, tenacious endurance, and unfailing skill – the will to summon the other boats to the attack, in addition to carrying out your own attack.

341.) In carrying out common operations against the enemy, there is no distinction between reconnaissance and attack. If, in certain circumstances, only one of these tasks can be carried out, the attack has unconditional priority.

Departures from this fundamental rule must be specially authorized in each individual case.

B. System of Command.

342.) The distribution and grouping of the submarine, and the operational and tactical command, is ordinarily in the hands of the Submarine Command ("B.d.U.").

Groups.

343.) If there is a considerable number of submarines, a subdivision in "submarine groups" may be made.

Group Commanders.

344.) When group commanders are appointed for this purpose by the Submarine Command, they assume the tactical direction of their groups. If no group commanders are appointed, the tactical command of the individual groups remains in the hands of the Submarine Command.

If a group commander is prevented from giving orders, and does not appear on the scene, his duties are taken over by the Submarine Command, unless a substitute has been specially appointed.

345.) The tactical command of the group commanders should be limited to taking steps to relocate the enemy, when contact has been lost; for example, by organizing reconnaissance or advance patrols.

The group commanders must send in a report to the Submarine Command, when the situation is such that it cannot be taken in by the command on land.

346.) An order issued by the Submarine Command overrides an order by a group commander.

[. . .]

C. Taking Up Action Stations: Method and Formation.
Formation.

349.) There is no hard and fast rule for the common attack.

To facilitate the direction of the operations, however, the following patterns have been fixed:

area of attack
action stations   in certain cases
waiting stations   with "centre of
reconnaissance patrol(s)   gravity"
advance patrol(s)

Positions occupied boat by boat.

350.) In all attack formations the positions are occupied singly (one boat at a time).

Area of attack.

351.) The area of attack is that part of the theater of operations of the submarines which is assigned to one submarine.

This method is adopted when large sea areas are to be patrolled and no precise data are available regarding the enemy traffic.

The area of attack of the individual submarine is defined in squares, latitude and longitude, or by other limits. If the areas of attack are defined as squares of a certain "depth," the term "depth" means the diameter of the area with the prescribed square as its center. Example: "Area of attack square X depth 20 sm" means: The area of attack is bounded by a circle with a radius of 10 sm about the center of the square X.

Freedom of movement, and Authority to attack in the area of attack.

352.) Within its allotted area each submarine has full freedom of movement, in order to seek its own targets. Every worthwhile target must be attacked.

Evacuation of the area of attack.

353.) The submarine must leave the area of attack:

a) for the purpose of attacking an enemy, and of prosecuting the attack (pursuing the enemy), if the submarine is *itself* in contact, or has been in contact, with the enemy;

b) for the purpose of carrying out independent operations against *convoys and concentrations of warships*, concerning which reports have been received from other submarines, or from the Submarine Command ("B.d.U."), if those convoys or warships are within reach.

On the completion of the attacks, the submarine must go back into the reconnaissance, area.

354.) A submarine may leave its area of attack when special circumstances, or particularly efficient counteraction of the enemy, make it impossible for it to stay there. The evacuation of the area of attack must then be reported as soon as possible.

[. . .]

Distribution of Action Stations.

356.) The object of the "distribution of action stations" is to contact a particular enemy unit, *which must be mentioned in the instructions (order)*.

Action stations are defined in the instructions (order) in squares of a certain depth (see No. 351) or other geographical points with a certain depth.

Taking up action stations.

357.) If the instructions issued by the Command do not provide for a special formation of the submarines, and for special positions, the positions are occupied in the order of the boat numbers, i.e., the submarine with the lowest number occupies the position first indicated, the submarine with the next lowest number the second position, and so on.

If the instructions specify a certain time of day, the positions should be taken up by that time.

Operating from action stations.

358.) The submarine must operate from the action station, against the target indicated in the instructions, as soon as the target is reported.

Authority to attack from action stations.

359.) Targets other than those mentioned in the instructions (order) should be attacked:
- when the attack on the main target is not thereby endangered;
- when a target is found which is approximately as valuable as the prescribed target;
- when the targets are warships from cruisers upwards.

Abandoning action stations.

360.) The action stations may be abandoned for the purpose of prosecuting the attack on these targets, if they have been sighted by the submarine itself, as well as in the cases defined in No. 354.

361.) Limitations or extensions of the authority to attack are provided for in the operational order.

[. . .]

Waiting Station.

364.) The "waiting station" is a preliminary position before taking up action stations. It is used when precise details of a given target are not available, and when the Submarine Command wishes to reserve its decision as regards the attack, after receiving reports about important targets.

The distributions and the taking up of "waiting stations" are subject to the same rules as apply to taking up action stations (see Nos. 356, 357).

Authority to attack from waiting station.

365.) Failing special orders, the boats are authorized to attack, from their waiting stations, any target approximately as valuable as the target of the submarines on action stations, warships from cruisers upwards, and other targets, if the attack on the latter does not interfere with the subsequent attack on the target prescribed for the submarines on "waiting station."

Abandoning the waiting station.

366.) A submarine may only abandon its waiting station:
- in the prosecution of an attack on one of the targets specified in No. 359, provided the submarine has itself made contact;
- on orders of the Submarine Command, or of a group commander who is authorized accordingly:
- in the cases mentioned in No. 354.

[. . .]

Center of gravity.

369.) If a "center of gravity" is provided for in the order, the submarine must operate, in the first place, round the "center of gravity." If they there encounter a strong defence, or see no chance of a successful attack, they may temporarily carry out raids in every direction within the boundaries of their areas, but they should always return afterwards to the "center of gravity."

Reconnaissance and Vanguard patrols ("A.St." or "Vp.St.").

370.) Reconnaissance and vanguard patrols are carried out for the purpose of patrolling large sea areas, with sound-location, as well as of contacting certain targets.

In the instructions (order) their patrols are identified by starting points and terminal points. The boat first mentioned in the order occupies the starting point, the boat last mentioned the terminal point. The other boats take up equidistant stations, in the sequence indicated in the order, between the starting point and the terminal point.

Advance and Direction of Advance of Reconnaissance Patrol.

371.) The direction and speed of advance of a reconnaissance patrol are given in the order as "course" and "speed." They should be adhered to as an average course and an average speed of the individual submarine in crossing the area.

If the order calls for an advance by position lines, the position lines must be reached at the prescribed times, after which the average course and speed of the individual submarine should be calculated with regard to the current, the motion of the sea, and the wind.

Vanguard patrols, in contradistinction to the reconnaissance patrols, do not change their stations.

The German U-boat *U-278*, its image captured during the overflight by a US B-24 Liberator.

Radius of Action of Reconnaissance Patrols and Advance Patrols.

372.) The reconnaissance area of the individual submarine on reconnaissance patrol and advance patrol, comprises the distance from the point computed for the individual boat, towards both sides in the direction of the patrol, to a point situated halfway between the submarine and the next I submarine; for the first and last boat, the reconnaissance area extends, by 1 half the distance of the space between the boats, beyond the starting and terminal points.

Vertically to the reconnaissance and advance patrols, there is in general no such thing as operational "depth," except insofar as it is necessary to enable the individual submarine to accomplish its tasks according to No. 373.

"Depth" in the area of the reconnaissance and advance patrols.

If, by way of exception, a "depth" is provided for in the instructions for the reconnaissance and advance patrols, the size of the reconnaissance area (reconnaissance range) of the individual submarine is adjusted according to No. 351.

[. . .]

D. How to act in the Area of Operation before and during Contact with the Enemy.
Remain invisible.

375.) It is a fundamental rule to remain unseen, in every position, until the submarine carries out its attack. 'Consequently, the action of the individual submarine is governed by the rules laid down in Section I, B.

Freedom of movement.

376.) Within the limits of their own areas, the submarines act on their own initiative. They should seek the most favorable conditions for attack, in accordance with the rules for the various positions, on the basis of their estimation of the position of the enemy, the defence, the state of the weather, and other circumstances. There is plenty of scope here for the penetration and skill of the commander.

Authority to attack.

377.) The authority to attack contained in the rules for taking up the different positions, means, at the same time, an order to attack.

In cases of genuine doubt, the commander must decide in favor of attacking. A successful attack is always a gain – a neglected opportunity cannot be made good.

General reports.

378.) In making reports, the commander must always ask himself the following questions:

a) To what extent is the command, and to what extent are the other submarines, informed of the position?

b) What do the command and the other submarines require to know about a new position?

c) Will the transmission of my message now and here be bad for any of the other boats? Is my message so important that I must accept that?

d) What else is there of importance to the command if I decide to send a message? For example, weather, shipping (naval) successes, fuel position, available torpedoes.

e) After formulating and before transmitting the message: have I expressed myself as briefly, and, above all, as clearly as possible, or may I be misunderstood?

379.) For the command, it is important to know exactly what clues the enemy may have to the positions of submarines.

Submarines which have undoubtedly been sighted by the enemy in the area of operations, must therefore report this by short signal.

[. . .]

Keeping the contact with important objectives.

382.) Without prejudice to the attack which the submarine has been detailed to carry out, which always has priority, the submarine must make contact with important objectives.

Important objectives are:

- Convoys
- Concentrations of Warships;
- the targets mentioned in the order to take up stations.

If contact is also to be maintained with other targets, and other submarines are to attack outside their own areas, instructions to this effect will be issued in the operation order, or in a special order.

If a submarine makes contact with an important enemy, all submarines within striking distance begin to cooperate – the great hour of the submarine commanders and crews.

CHAPTER 5
DEFENSIVE ACTIONS

During World War II, the field of anti-submarine warfare progressed every bit as quickly as – if not quicker than – innovations in submarine technology. These advances were especially rapid in the Atlantic theatre, as the British and the Americans sought every possible means to defeat the German U-boat threat, a goal that by mid-1944 they had largely achieved. From a technological point of view, some of the most significant steps forward included the use of ASDIC/Sonar detection, the fitting of high-frequency direction finding (HF/DF) and centimetric radar sets to both aircraft and submarines (dramatically improving submarine detection rates), magnetic anomaly detection (MAD) devices, improved depth-charge systems, and the introduction of ultra-long-range air patrols to close the "mid-Atlantic gap" in which U-boats previously operated without overhead threats. But these innovations in weapon systems were bolstered by other factors, such as the huge advances the Allies made in breaking German naval intelligence codes, the effective use of the convoy system, improved escort tactics, the vast industrial output of "Liberty" merchant ships from US dockyards and the capturing the enemy submarine bases through land advances.

It was all these effects, plus many others, taken together that ultimately made the oceans such a dangerous place for submarine crews, not just German crews in the Atlantic but crews of all nationalities in the various theatres around the world. Survival in such a hostile environment to a large degree depended on the defensive intelligence of the submarine's commander, and this chapter looks squarely at the subject of submarine defence, both in terms of preventing attacks in the first place through to how to survive persistent and heavy assault by aircraft or surface vessels. We start with a section from The Fleet *Type Submarine*, which explains the principles of how to maintain effective watches. For in the cat-and-mouse game of submarine vs. enemy, the crew who spotted the opponent first was the most likely to survive the day.

The Fleet Type Submarine (1946)

PATROL ROUTINE

A. INTRODUCTION

20A1. Foreword. The following patrol instructions are a compilation of instructions used by various submarines. Naturally, there may be some minor differences between these instructions and those used by a particular submarine.

B. DUTIES OF WATCH STANDERS

20B1. Officer of the deck. On the surface, the officer of the deck stands his watch in the forward bridge structure. Although he is expected to remain intensely alert and observant, he is not a lookout and must not become engrossed in a detail of his watch or a lookout sector to the exclusion of his comprehensive duties as supervisor of the watch. His responsibility when the ship is submerged is no less than when on the surface. and a similar degree of alertness is required in carrying out the routine and direction of the watch. The duties of the officer of the deck as outlined in Navy Regulations, are supplemented as follows:

Keep the number of persons on the bridge to a minimum, requiring permission to come on the bridge in each case.

Allow only one relief of any watch on the bridge at a time, with the exception that besides one lookout relieving, the quarter master or junior officer of the deck may relieve.

Insure yourself that the lookout's vision has become dark-adapted before allowing him to relieve the watch. A reasonable test is the lookout's ability at a distance of about 5 feet to note how many fingers you have extended.

Keep the lookouts alert and insure that they are properly covering their sectors. Insist on standard phraseology in all reports, with prompt acknowledgments. Maintain the passageway to the hatch clear at all times.

Insure that the quartermaster orders rain clothes for the watch in sufficient time to permit one person at a time to don them prior to arrival of a squall. Place the lookouts where they will be of most advantage.

Keep them as dry as possible and out of high wind. A comfortable lookout is much more efficient than an uncomfortable one.

The following rules apply generally, but in no way restrict the officer of the deck from acting as his judgment dictates:

Dive for all aircraft contacts, except as specifically directed by previous instructions of the commanding officer.

Turn toward a periscope forward of the beam and go to full speed. Turn away from a periscope abaft the beam and go to full speed.

Turn away from all fishing vessels or small craft unless ordered by the commanding officer to attack.

Turn away from unidentifiable objects.

Turn toward a target, but dive in sufficient time to insure that your ship is not sighted prior to firing torpedoes.

Present the smallest target possible by turning toward or away from any type of contact as the situation dictates.

In friendly waters, or when contact with own forces is probable, have daily recognition signals written in chalk on wind screen.

Know and insure that all bridge personnel on watch know the current signals in effect, and that recognition gear is in complete readiness as follows:

1. Searchlight tested if rigged.
2. Blinker tube readily accessible.
3. Flares and rockets changed at proper times.

Carry out the following details or routine:

Approximately 15 minutes before diving secure the 20-mm guns and ammunition.

Carry out the diving procedure.

After daylight and torpedo routining, the depth at which to run during and between looks will depend on the state of the sea and the proximity of enemy air bases, as directed by the commanding officer.

When landmarks are available, keep the ship's position cut in, using periscope exposures of short duration only.

In making periscope observations, first sweep the horizon and sky in low power for aircraft or close surface craft. Follow this, if all clear, by a slow deliberate search in high power, not exposing the periscope for more than 15 seconds. Develop the habit of obtaining a complete picture of the weather during your observation. Have the quartermaster note the keel depth during the observation and also tell you when 15 seconds of periscope exposure has occurred.

When the target is sighted, sound the general alarm, or pass the word over the telephone if the target is likely to hear the alarm, and commence the approach immediately. Minutes or seconds may be just as valuable then as later in the attack, and certainly are if the target is presenting a large angle on the bow.

Habitually require a smart trim from your diving officer for the depth at which you are running.

Notify the commanding officer when darkness is almost ready to set in and obtain the time of surfacing from him. Commence the surfacing procedure.

Ten minutes prior to surfacing, the commanding officer comes to the conning tower and relieves the watch. The junior officer of the deck of the previous watch relieves the diving officer a half hour prior to surfacing. Normally, just prior to surfacing, the ship is brought to 50 feet for SD sweep, then to 40 feet for SJ sweep (sound sweeping all the time).

If "All clear on radar" is indicated, pass. the work over the loudspeaker, "Stand by to surface .... engine combination." The commanding officer will then direct the surface alarm be sounded.

Carry out surfacing procedure on the surface, alarm.

Obtain the commanding officer's permission prior to the following:

1. Permitting anyone on deck.
2. Putting any piece of machinery or armament out of commission.
3. Pulling a torpedo from any tube.
4. Anything that may reduce the fighting ability of the ship or her ability to dive.

For every sighting while on the surface that might develop into an attack, sound the general alarm and let the rest of the ship know something is happening.

Whenever the need arises to make ready torpedoes, order "Make ready tubes forward (or aft)."

Keep the junior officer of the deck informed of changes of speed, course, or any other pertinent information so that he will be able to assume the deck at any time.

20B2. Junior officer of the deck. The junior officer of the deck stands his watch as directed by the commanding officer. He may act in any one of three capacities as follows:

As junior officer of the deck, stationed forward or aft the cigarette deck. (If aft, quartermaster should go forward.)

As junior officer of the deck, stationed in the conning tower.

The junior officer of the deck watch normally is stood only while on the surface. Until all officers are fully qualified as diving officer, the junior officer of the deck normally acts as diving officer submerged. However, if qualified by the commanding officer, he may interchange with the OOD for periscope watches if practicable.

Duties of the junior officer of the deck are as follows:

Supervise the lookouts to insure that they are covering their sectors properly.

Observe to insure that any enemy that might possibly get by the lookouts does not approach, unobserved, to close range. (If forward, observe from broad on opposite bow to stern.)

Note the condition of the 20-mm guns and be prepared to man or direct the fire as directed by the OOD.

Report immediately to the officer of the deck own engine smoke, sparks, or any unusual condition.

Proceed to diving station or below on orders of the officer of the deck or on "Clear the bridge." Carry out the diving procedure. Conduct the periscope watch as directed. Man the TDC and otherwise assist the OOD in conducting initial stages of any approach as directed.

The junior officer of the deck should be fully aware of the condition of the boat and prepared to assume the capacity of the officer of the deck at any time.

20B3. Conning tower talker watch. The conning tower talker watch is normally stood at all times when at sea. Conning tower talker watches are stood as indicated on the Watch, Quarter, and Station bill.

The duties of this watch may be outlined as follows:

Instruct new steersmen in their duties.

Make all necessary entries in the Quartermaster Notebook.

Act as voice link between sound, radar, control, maneuvering, and bridge watches.

Supervise zig plan if in use.

Take and record TBT and heading bearings on bridge buzzer marks.

Act as telephone watch.

Keep conning tower clear of loose gear.

Under supervision of the chief petty officer of the watch, permit but one relief for any watch to proceed to the bridge.

At night, check and carry out the night orders.

Upon surfacing, check TBT's with the quartermaster as directed.

Assist the quartermaster in maintaining deck log columns.

Maintain quiet in the conning tower and keep an alert watch. Report to the OOD when the conning tower watch is properly relieved.

Know exactly where all the conning tower alarms are and operate them only when ordered to do so by the bridge.

20B4. The steersman. The steersman is normally stationed in the conning tower, unless otherwise ordered by the officer of the deck.

The duties of the steersman are as follows:

Maintain the course.

Operate the maneuvering room annunciators as ordered by the bridge.

Know the duties of the conning tower watch.

Assist the conning tower watch as necessary and be able to take over at any time.

Know exactly where all conning tower alarms are and operate them only when ordered to do so by the bridge.

20B5. Quartermaster of the watch. The quartermaster of the watch normally is stationed on the bridge, aft when cruising, and may exchange with the OOD if ordered. He is an additional all-around lookout and does not restrict his search to any one sector unless so ordered by the officer of the deck.

The quartermaster is responsible under the direction of the OOD for the following routine duties:

Break out binoculars, dark glasses, proper flares, and blinker tube prior to surfacing; also issue lens paper to lookouts.

Obtain warmer clothing or rain clothing for lookouts.

Change flares at the proper time.

Check TBT's upon surfacing each night.

Wipe the periscope windows on surfacing and 15 minutes before routine dives.

Operate the periscope, keep the periscope officer informed of depth, and read and record bearings when submerged.

Keep the conning tower clean, and all gear properly stowed when submerged.

Check columns of deck log after being relieved to make sure that the proper entries have been made. Do this in the control room.

Once every hour on surface, check the lookouts' glasses for cleanliness and proper setting.

20B6. Chief petty officer of the watch. The CPO of the watch remains in the control room. He is charged with running the below deck routine, supervising the control room watch when on the surface, and with carrying out the details of the Watch Bill. He initiates the diving diving officer. In carrying out his duties, he must pay particular attention to the following:

Call the oncoming watch in sufficient time for them to relieve 15 minutes before the hour, in accordance with naval custom.

At night, insure that each oncoming lookout is fitted with and wears dark adaptation goggles continuously for at least 20 minutes before being allowed to proceed to the conning tower.

Insure that only one relief proceeds to the conning tower at a time.

Promptly acknowledge any orders or word passed from the bridge or conning tower.

Periodically check the compensation by liquidometer gages.

Insure that the proper watch is maintained on the control room (SD) radar when ordered manned, and that any contact, however doubtful, is reported instantly to the, OOD.

Maintain quiet and allow no loitering in the control room.

Half an hour prior to surfacing, rig the hatch skirt. Turn out the white lights; turn on the red as designated for the control room.

Execute the 2200 lights out in the crew's Mess.

At the end of each watch, and approximately 1 hour before diving, pump the bilges and blow the sanitary tanks to the sea.

Keep the manometer needles matched on surface.

Keep submerged identification signal available as directed by OOD.

Maintain the air banks at proper pressure.

See that all the topside reliefs are properly clothed.

Keep the control room clear of all loose gear.

About 1 hour before surfacing when directed by the OOD, pump down the pressure in the boat to one-tenth.

After surfacing, carry out the evening routine which consists of the following:

1. After the blowers are secured, start air change.
2. Pump all the bilges to the sea.
3. Blow all the sanitary tanks.

4. Collect all trash and garbage and when properly sacked, report to the bridge, "All trash and garbage assembled," and dump it when directed.

Carry out evening compensation as directed by the diving officer.

When orders to the steersman for changes of course or speed come from the bridge over the system, observe the motor order telegraph repeater or rudder angle indicator in the control room to check that the order is being carried out properly.

Keep the compass check book, making entries as required by the navigator. Instructions will be posted in the front of the book. While submerged, whenever word is passed from the conning tower, "Man battle stations," dispatch one man forward and one man aft with the order, "Pass word quietly, wake all hands. Battle stations submerged."

20B7. Lookouts. Normally there are three lookouts assigned overlapping sectors as follows:

Starboard lookout 350 degrees – 130 degrees (relative).

After lookout 120 degrees – 240 degrees (relative).

Port lookout 230 degrees – 010 degrees (relative).

In the event that four lookouts are used, sectors are assigned as follows:

Starboard forward lookout 350 degrees – 100 degrees (relative).

Starboard after lookout 080 degrees – 190 degrees (relative)

Port after lookout 170 degrees – 280 degrees (relative).

Port forward lookout 010 degrees – 260 degrees (relative).

During daylight, each lookout searches his sector in the following sequence using a sun filter only when searching into the sun:

a. Search the water to the horizon for one-half of his assigned sector.

b. Lower the binoculars for approximately 10 seconds to survey entire sector, water, and sky, with naked eye. Continue search of water to horizon over the remainder of the sector. Search the horizon and lower sky for one-half of the assigned sector. Lower binoculars for approximately 10 seconds to survey the entire sector, water and sky with the naked eye. Continue search of the horizon and lower sky over the remainder of the sector. Repeat 10-second sweep of the entire sector with naked eye. Search the upper sky, above the belt observed when searching the horizon and lower sky, for one-half of assigned sector. Lower binoculars for approximately 10 seconds to survey the entire sector, water and sky, with naked eye. Continue search of upper sky for remainder of sector. Repeat 10-second sweep of entire sector with naked eye. Recommence, starting with (a) above.

During darkness, the search will be as follows:

The view of a US submarine conning tower in 1945, with crew members standing watch.

a. Moonlight nights when enemy air search is possible: After each complete sweep of sector, search sky sector with naked eye.

b. Dark nights: Eliminate sky search.

This method of search has the following advantages:

It provides a systematic coverage of the entire area.

It gives maximum insurance against any plane, which was outside the field of the binoculars, closing unobserved to close range.

Provides best assurance that a periscope lowered during the binocular search, will be sighted if dangerously close during the naked eye sweeps.

General instructions to lookouts:

Save your eyes. All lookouts should rest their eyes before coming on watch. They should try to take care of all calls of nature before going on watch.

If a lookout does not feel physically up to standing an all-out lookout watch, he should report this to the OOD.

Make all reports of sightings immediately. It is better to be wrong 100 times than miss one ship.

Use relative bearings in all reports. Then, followed by your best estimate of the range, add more information as it becomes available, stating identity of ship and so forth.

Call out your reports so that all can hear. Make certain your report is acknowledged and keep on reporting until you get an acknowledgment.

Do not take eyes or binoculars off the object you have sighted.

Report everything.

Upon assuming your post after surfacing, make a complete search of your sector. Report in a loud clear voice, "......... sector all clear, sir."

At night, don't attempt night duties until dark-adapted; avoid short cuts. Practice use of the corners of the eyes, remembering that objects are better seen in dim light if not located in the center of vision. Move the eyes frequently, remembering that night vision is most sensitive immediately after the line of sight has been shifted. When relieving, make certain that no other bridge watch is being relieved, then request, "Permission to come on the bridge to relieve lookout." Relieve with a minimum of noise and confusion. Get dressed below for the existing weather conditions.

20B8. Sound watch.

a. General. The sound watch normally is stood whenever speed conditions permit. The operator must, without seeking confirmation or help from anyone, report immediately to the officer of the deck any echo ranging, propellers, or unusual sounds.

b. Instructions for standing sound watches. The safety of the ship and its personnel is directly dependent upon the manner in which this watch is stood. This responsibility is greatly increased at night and a resultant increase in attentiveness is imperative.

This watch must be stood in regulation manner. Submerged, each man upon being relieved reports to the officer of the deck, "Sound watch relieved by ...., Sound conditions are (good, fair, poor)." On Surface, report to the conning tower talker that you have been properly relieved.

Soundheads are to be used in accordance with communication officer orders posted at the sound gear.

If for any reason, you have difficulty interpreting what you hear, or the equipment does not appear to be operating correctly, inform the officer of the deck at once, and call for one of the battle station soundmen at the same time without any further orders.

c. Additional information regarding night sound, watches. Soundheads should not be left lowered above 10 knots.

When two soundmen are on watch at the same time, both soundheads are lowered. The starboard (JK) operator covers the sector from zero to 180, and the port (CQ) operator covers the sector from 180 to 360.

Each soundhead should be rotated 360 degrees on alternate sweeps.

If screws are heard, they are to be reported immediately, stating "Screws at .... relative, (high or low) speed." Then obtain the closest true bearing and report, "True bearing ...." Thereafter, report any change in speed of screws, and if you can no longer hear them. Changes of bearing when own ship is on a steady course are very important. Keep the information coming.

We now return to the *U-boat Commander's Handbook*, beginning with a section on 'How to Prevent the Submarine from Attracting Attention'. This activity alone must have taken up a decent portion of a submarine captain's mental capacity. The intensity of overhead sunshine, the salinity of the water, the colour of the sea bed, the making of radio transmissions, the wake of a raised periscope, the effects of fluorescent algae at night, enemy aerial observation – dozens of environmental, operational and technical factors influenced the chances of a submarine being detected by the enemy. Make a mistake in just one area, and the result might be the sudden appearance of an anti-submarine aircraft or destroyer, attacking as if out of nowhere.

The most nail-biting experience of all would be attempting to escape detection and attack by an enemy already alert to the submarine's presence. The submarine commander would have to use all his guile and "reading" of enemy intentions to slip the net of detection, an activity often conducted to the eerie "ping" of ASDIC emanating from the ships above. ASDIC was an acronym of Allied Submarine Detection Investigation Committee, although in US use it was also known as Sonar, from SOund Navigation And Ranging. ASDIC/Sonar was a system that emitted regular pulses of sound through the water, and if a pulse hit a submerged object, it would bounce back to a receiver station, providing the operator with enough information to ascertain range and bearing to the submarine, which would then be attacked. The submarine commander's job was both to escape from this technological snare, while also outwitting increasingly experienced escort captains, who would be attempting to second guess the submarine commander's movements. It was a game played for the highest stakes, and requiring exceptional mental resilience, as the fight could be conducted over many hours, even days. For those above, the main evidence that they had achieved a kill would be a large patch of oil forming on the surface.

U-boat Commander's Handbook (1943)

B. How to Prevent the Submarine from Attracting Attention.

19.) The chief value of the submarine is its characteristic ability, which it possesses in an exceptional degree, to attack without being seen, and thus to achieve the element of surprise. The precondition of success is surprise. If the submarine is seen by the enemy, it is deprived of almost every chance of success. The commander of the submarine must therefore make every effort to preserve the paramount advantage of surprise, as far as it is at all possible.

20.) In order to remain undetected, before and during the attack, the submarine must be neither sighted, nor sound-located, nor detected by ASDIC.

I. Action to be Taken by the Submarine, in Order not to be Spotted.

21.) In every situation, both on passage (or approach) and in launching the attack, the submarine must be guided by the motto: "He who sees first, has won!" Untiring vigilance of the look-out involves success and safety of the submarine, and is, therefore, at one and the same time, a means attack and defence.

Consequently, when operating on the surface, a sharp lookout should always be kept, systematically organized in sectors (examination of the horizon for ships, of the surrounding surface of the sea for periscopes, and of the sky for aircraft). The most dangerous enemy of the submarine is the aircraft, by reason of its great speed. Consequently, during daylight and on moonlit nights, the sky should be watched with special care.

22.) To keep a conscientious lookout tiring; consequently, the look-out should be punctually and frequently relieved. Sunglasses should be held in readiness for all members of the watch.

Particular attention should be paid to the sun sector, in order to be safe sudden air attack.

23.) The periscope should not be used in daylight, on the surface, except special circumstances (for example, in remote sea areas; also as under No. 24). It is the raised periscope on the surface that makes the typical submarine silhouette. Similarly, on submerging in daylight, the periscope should not be raised until the submarine is well below the surface. In the same way, the submarine should not surface during the day, before the periscope has been lowered.

24.) If, for urgent reasons, such as overhauling, it should become imperatively necessary to raise the periscope by day when the submarine is on the surface, the additional height of the raised periscope can be used in suitable weather to send up a look-out with binoculars, provided that surprise attacks by hostile airplanes are not to be anticipated. If the weather clear and the sea calm, advantage can be taken of the raising of the periscope, for an all-round view. On account of the relatively week magnification of the periscope, however, and of the almost inevitable vibrations and movement of the vessel, this seldom serves a useful purpose. The danger of betraying oneself by the raised periscope is greater.

25.) In clear weather, do not allow yourself to be seen on the dip of the horizon. Submerge, at the latest, when the top of the funnel of the sighted

A U-boat radio petty officer, sitting in his booth, checks the area around the boat for sounds.

ship is visible in the dip of the horizon. Some warships, besides having lookout posts with binoculars on the mast, have range finders of great optical efficiency in the foretop. In clear weather, therefore, one should never be able to see more of the enemy than the tops of his masts. Anyone who can see more – i.e., who approaches nearer – automatically runs the danger of being sighted, himself, by the enemy.

It is better to submerge too soon than too late, and thus lose one's chance altogether. The limits of what is possible in various kinds of weather can only be learned by experience.

The look-out on merchant ships, and the danger of being sighted at night, are easily overestimated.

26.) If there is a danger of surprise attacks in sea areas efficiently patrolled hostile planes and warships, and especially if the submarine is engaged operations there that require it to be stationary, it must remain underwater from dawn to dusk.

27.) It may also be advisable to remain submerged in misty or foggy weather. In poor visibility, the approach of ships can be more easily detected underwater [from the sound of the ships' engines] by means of the hydrophone, than on the surface by the look-out.

28.) This possibility of using the hydrophone to help in detecting surf ships should, however, be restricted to those cases in which the submarine is unavoidably compelled to stay below the surface. The hydrophone must not lead to inactivity [passivity] underwater, which would be wrong; it is an auxiliary instrument and no more, and can never be a substitute for ocular perception and surface viewing. As soon as visibility allows, the, place of the submarine is on the surface. Otherwise valuable opportunities of attack are lost.

29.) The danger of a surprise attack exists, in particular, when the submarine comes to the surface, especially after traveling long distances at considerable depth. When coming up from a considerable depth, an all-round sound location should therefore be carried out at a safe depth, where the submarine cannot be rammed; i.e., at a depth of approximately 20 m, at "sound-location speed." Next, the submarine should go rapidly through the danger zone at periscope depth, with the periscope raised; careful all-round look-out with and without magnification – submersion up to 9 m, depending on the weather, then lower the periscope altogether (see No. 23) and surface at high speed. The manhole of the conning tower is opened as quickly as possible, and the commander – with, at the most, one man who is especially good as a look-out – goes up. It is not until the surface of the sea has again been examined with binoculars, in every direction, that the compressed air cells can be completely emptied of water.

30.) By careful supervision, the submarine should be prevented from leaving traces of oil (leaking oil tanks, etc.). Patches of oil may also be left behind when submerging, as a result of a residue of air in the compressed air cells. Consequently, the submarine should not remain near the place where it has submerged.

31.) After the submarine has submerged, the periscope can be shown in a low position, and left there, up to a distance of approximately 4 to 5,000 m from the enemy, according to the state of the weather.

At lesser distances, the "sparing" use of the periscope begins, that is to say, the periscope is frequently and intermittently shown, each time for a little while, in a very low position where it is almost always awash, while the submarine travels at low speed.

For rules for the use of the periscope when attacking, see Section II, C, No. 125.

32.) For the color of the periscope, a dull, dirty grey such as is used for the body of the submarine itself should be chosen, as this color is the least easy to detect in all conditions of light. Green paint, or stripes or checkered patterns, are very conspicuous in a poor light.

33.) Every aircraft sighted should be regarded as hostile until the contrary is proved.

34.) Submarines on the surface are not easily detected from an aircraft when the sea is rough, unless seen in their characteristic outline against the dip of the horizon. If the sea is calm, the track (wake) of the submarine is usually seen first from the plane, especially if the submarine is moving at speed.

35.) The submarine must endeavor to keep a sufficiently sharp look-out to be able to see the aircraft before it is spotted by the latter. It is then master of the situation, and will soon learn to decide whether it must submerge, or can remain on the surface; if it is not certain that the latter can be done, it is better to reduce the chances of success by a premature temporary submersion, or a retreat to greater depths to avoid being spotted by the aircraft, than to spoil the chance altogether by being spotted.

36.) In good visibility, it is possible to sight the plane in time. It is consequently right to remain on the surface in areas threatened from the air, and to keep the area under observation. More can be seen above water and below. In addition, by remaining below, valuable opportunities of attack may be lost.

37.) Conditions are different, in particular, in areas threatened from the air, when the submarine is engaged in operations that cause it to remain stationary in misty weather, with poor visibility and low clouds. In such circumstances it is right to remain submerged during the day, because, if it has surfaced, the submarine may easily be surprised by aircraft suddenly appearing in near sight, without being able to submerge in time, and reach safety.

38.) The submerged submarine is most difficult to spot from the plane when all its horizontal surfaces are painted very dark. All other bright objects on the upper deck, as, for example, the insulators of the net wire, must have a coating of dark paint. In case of need, paint which has crumbled, or been washed off during the operations, must be replaced; for is purpose, a quantity of dark paint should always be available during operations.

39.) A submarine painted in this way can only be spotted by an airplane, if the submarine is submerged,

a) when the sun is shining, and the sunlight penetrates the water below the surface; without the sun, the water is a dark mass, which hides all objects from view;

b) when the surface of the sea is not so rough – approximately from motion [sea] 2 to 3 upwards--- that the continuous refraction makes it impossible to see below the surface, even when the sun is shining;

c) when the airplane is almost vertically above the submarine. Because of the high speed of the airplane, it is very difficult to spot a submarine moving under water.

The conditions described above – sun, rough sea, position of the aircraft in relation to the submerged submarine – are relatively more favorable or unfavorable for the airplanes in sea areas with exceptionally clear, or exceptionally turbid, water, for example, in the Mediterranean, and in the Baltic at the mouths of rivers. In sea areas where the water is clear, so that it is correspondingly easier to look into it from airplanes directly above, the submarine must therefore submerge, in good time, to a greater depth, in order not to be spotted.

40.) Even when the submarine is not traveling at speed, if the sea is smooth, the tracks [wake] of the screw [propeller] of the vessel, and of the periscope, may betray the submarine to the airplane. When there is a danger of air attack in such conditions, the submarine should therefore submerge in good time, diving to a considerable depth, except when the sky is kept under observation through the periscope.

[. . .]

II. Principles of Defence by Means of Sound Location.

46.) The underwater torpedo attack of the submarine without warning is bound up with defence against sound location of the enemy.
The efficiency of the enemy sound location depends on:

    a) the efficiency of the sound locator (hydrophone),

    b) the acoustical conductivity of the water,

    c) the interference level of the sound-locating vessel,

    d) the volume of the sound to be located.

47.) The efficiency of the various types of enemy sound locators (hydrophones) is not known. In estimating it, we can assume that it is similar to that of our own sound locating instruments.

48.) The acoustical conductivity of the water depends on the uniformity of its condition. Differences of temperature and salt content – that is to say, in the different layers of the water which are caused by currents, tides, and the motion of the sea – reduce the conductivity of the water. The same result is brought about by permeation of the water with air, or with plankton containing air. Uniformly high or uniformly low temperatures, as well as uniformly high or uniformly low proportions of salt in the water, increase the conductivity. In the Baltic and the North Sea, conditions are generally bad for sound locating; in other words, favorable for submarines.

49.) The interference level of the sound-locating vessel depends on the magnitude of the sounds proceeding from it, and on the state of the sea. Traveling at speed, and rough seas, as well as the proximity of other ships, greatly impair the efficiency of the sound locating instruments.

50.) The magnitude of the sounds originating in the submerged submarine can be greatly reduced by traveling at "sound location speed." The degree of speed most favorable for sound location, and the magnitudes of the sounds originating in the individual machines, engines [motors], and instruments, may be different in each individual boat, and must be determined by sound locating tests. The procedure appropriate to each submarine, when traveling at "sound location speed," must be determined by the result of these tests.

a) low speed: the revolutions must in this case be determined by the sound locating tests, and must in certain circumstances be different for each screw;

b) maximum silence of the crew in the submarine; speaking in low tones, working noiselessly; all auxiliary machines, etc., stopped, as far as they can be dispensed with.

In our waters, with their usually irregular layers, a submarine traveling at "sound location speed" can in general hardly be detected even by a slowly moving vessel pursuing it by sound location. In parts of the ocean with a better acoustic conductivity, conditions are more favorable for the enemy; in such sea areas the submarine should therefore take all precautions when traveling at "sound location speed."

[. . .]

III. Principles of Position Finding (ASDIC).

55.) To enable the underwater torpedo attack to be carried out without warning, it is further necessary that the submarine shall not be located by ASDIC.

The premises of the efficiency of the enemy defence based on ASDIC are the same as for sound location (see Nos. 46 to 54), viz.:

a) the efficiency of the submarine detecting gear,

b) the conditions for ASDIC resulting from the capacity of the water for transmitting the waves (rays) of the echo sounder,

c) the interference level of the hunting vessel,

d) the size of the echo-sounding surface of the target.

56.) The efficiency of enemy submarine detecting gear cannot yet be finally judged by experience so far gained during the war. It appears, however, that we have to reckon with submarine detecting gear of a performance equal to that of our "S" equipment.

a) The success of the ASDIC operations depends on the strength of the echo. Experience gained with our "S" equipment shows that the volume of the echo depends on the depth reached by the submerged target of the ASDIC operations, and that it frequently decreases in proportion as the depth of the target increases. In certain cases it will therefore be possible, by intercepting the enemy's echo impulses, and observing their strength (amplitude), to determine the most favorable depth. The weaker the reception of the echo impulses, the weaker the echo received by the enemy.

b) The echo impulses can be heard with both the "Hand K.D.B." and the "G.H.G." ("G" Sound Locator and/or "G" Hydrophone). In the case of the "G.H.G.," the high frequency filter should be used; that is to say, low sound frequencies should be cut out.

c) According to the experiences so far gained of the acoustical perception of the enemy's submarine detecting gear, we have to reckon with different kinds of echo impulses: in part, similar impulses to those of our own "S" equipment, but deeper in tone, in part, a constant humming. On several occasions, both sounds were audible, not only in the sound locator (hydrophone) but also everywhere in the vessel. Other experiences show that the enemy echo impulses resemble the ticking of a clock, or the tone of the "Atlas" echo sounder, and in other cases a tone increasing and decreasing in volume, which is a good direction finding target (bearing target), or that they resemble metallic blows on the sides of the submarine.

Among the manifestations of sound which resemble those of our "S" equipment, an interval of the impulses of 7 seconds has several times been unmistakably observed.

d) According to the experience so far gained, and the reports received, the submarine detecting gear used by the enemy seems, more especially, to supply exact particulars of depth.

57.) As regards the conditions of ASDIC in relation to the transmitting capacity of the water, it has been ascertained that the efficiency of the submarine-detecting gear is considerably reduced in sea areas with numerous layers of water.

a) Formation of layers of varying density ("stratification") of the water of the sea occurs after a long spell of sunshine on a calm sea, and also in a high degree in places where there is a mingling of different kinds of water, for example, at the confluence of the brackish waters of the Baltic with the salt water of the North Sea, in the Skagerrak and Kattegat; also in the Straits of Gibraltar, and on the confines of the Gulf Stream, in the Gulf Stream itself, near the mouths of rivers, and in other places (see Atlas of Water Densities of the Oceans). These "stratifications" of the water bring about a deflection of the wave of the echo sounder, so that the echo does not return to the receiver. In these circumstances, the submarine detecting gear does not function at all, or only for very short distances.

According to this, it is to be assumed, that the submarine detecting equipment of the enemy is frequently less efficacious in summer than in winter, and that this also applies to waters with a marked "stratification" (Skagerrak, Kattegat, West Coast of Norway, Pentland Firth, vicinity of the Gulf Stream, Straits of Gibraltar). Continual observation and measuring of water densities and temperatures are therefore important and indispensable, for establishing the presence of "stratification" when submerging to considerable depths as a means of evading pursuit by position finding.

A view of German submarine U-210 manoeuvering at full speed on the surface in a desperate and ultimately unsuccessful attempt to evade destruction by HMCS *Assiniboine* on 6 August 1942.

b) In addition, position finding is very difficult, and almost impossible, in shallow water of varying depths (sand banks), where there are many wrecks, as well as in narrow bays (Norwegian fjords), as it is usually not an echo that is produced, but numerous echoes, which make it difficult to keep, but more especially to locate, the target,

58.) The interference level of the hunting vessel is determined – also in hydrophone (sound locator) reception – by its wake, and by the state of the sea. High speed of the hunting vessel, and rough seas, limit the efficiency of the submarine detecting gear, or make it impossible to get results, because of the extensive permeation of the water with air in the neighborhood of the ship. For this reason, the conditions for hunting are usually unfavorable in the stern sector of the hunting vessel, as a result of the disturbance of the water by the propeller.

59.) The size of the echo-sounding surface of the target is of decisive importance for the strength of the echo.

a) If the submarine is broadside on in relation to the hunting ship, it will be more easily located than when it shows the narrow silhouette. Consequently, it is a matter of principle to show the narrow silhouette when being pursued by ASDIC. It is then, generally speaking, and as long as the submarine is not traveling at speed, immaterial whether the bows or the stern are turned toward the pursuer. The narrow silhouette over the bows is better, because, in the forward direction, the conditions are more advantageous for the submarine in regard to sound location by direction finding (bearing) and observation of echo impulses.

b) The behavior of the submarine when pursued by ASDIC is in other respects dictated by the same principles as apply to pursuit by sound location, viz.: maximum silence on board, since the submarine detecting gear is, or may be, suitable for use as a receiver for the ASDIC impulses.

[. . .]

Section IV
Action to be taken in case of Defensive Action and Pursuit by the Enemy.

246.) The object of the enemy anti-submarine defence and offensive action is the destruction of the submarine, either by direct armed attack underwater, or by keeping the submarine underwater to the point of exhaustion, and then destroying it when it surfaces.

247.) As a matter of principle, the submarine which is the object of enemy underwater pursuit should behave in such a way that it remains active, and should try to make good its escape by availing itself of every possibility, instead of simply waiting, and lying passively at the bottom. Activity on the part of the submarine always offers the best chances of shaking off the enemy.

248.) In all operations, the chief danger for the submarine is at the beginning, when the enemy, having witnessed the attack by the submarine, and seen it submerge, is best able to assess its position, and the submarine has not yet reached any great depth.

Consequently, if the submarine has been detected, it should leave the scene of the attack, or the spot where it has submerged, at full speed, and go deep down without troubling about the possibility of being sound-located.

[. . .]

A. What to do when pursued by Sound Location.

250.) Attention is called to the general remarks concerning enemy sound location: Section I, B, II, Nos. 46 to 54.

Suggestions as to the possibilities of shaking off the enemy:

a) Take the D/F sound location of the enemy astern.

b) Eliminate all sources of noise in the submarine: stop all auxiliary machinery which is not indispensable (pumps, ventilators, compressors, periscope motor, gyroscopic compass – above all, the secondary gyroscopes – etc.); main rudder and hydroplane should be operated by hand; pumping out,

Photos of an attack of two US Navy Grumman TBF *Avenger* aircraft on the German Type VIIC submarine *U-569* on 22 May 1943, in the North Atlantic. The submarine had to be scuttled after being badly damaged by depth charges; 21 sailors were killed aboard.

and trimming, with air; depth steering as far as possible only by head list, and then trimming by hand.

c) Absolute silence of the crew on board the submarine; speaking in low tones, working silently, moving about in stockinged feet, etc.

d) Go down very deep; the deeper the position of the submarine, the greater the probability of being incorrectly sound-located.

e) Run out and double at a good distance, and then make off on a straight course, in order to get well away from the pursuing enemy forces. Do not double frequently, or continually zigzag, because this results in loss of distance.

f) If possible, get away in the wake of the enemy's screw, on account of the effective interference level affecting his reception in sound location.

g) Accelerate your speed when the enemy accelerates (or when depth charges are detonated), and stop, or slow down to minimum r.p.m. of the engine, when the enemy stops.

[. . .]

B. What to do in Case of Pursuit by ASDIC.

254.) Attention is called to the general remarks about anti-submarine position finding: Section I, B, III, Nos. 55 to 64.

Measures to be taken against anti-submarine position finding:

a) Show the narrow outline (see No. 59) in order to offer the minimum echo sounding surface.

b) Go low down, and during the dive carry out consecutive measurements of the density and temperature of the water, with a view to ascertaining which stratum of water affords protection against the enemy ASDIC operations – a condition characterized by a weakening of the echo impulses (see No. 56, a and b). The weaker the reception of the echo impulses in the hydrophone of the submarine, the weaker, and therefore the more inaccurate, the echo returning to the enemy's submarine-detecting gear.

In certain circumstances, a temporary stationing of the submarine on the bottom of the sea is also likely to be successful as a protective measure against depth position finding operations of the enemy. This course can be particularly effective at great depths, because difference of depth of 6 to 8 m are then very hard to determine by means of the anti-submarine detecting gear.

c) Absolute silence of the crew on board the submarine (see No. 59, b, No. 250, b and c), on account of the possibility of detecting noises in the submarine through the medium of the enemy's anti-submarine gear.

d) Run out to a good distance, and double – no frequent zigzagging – and then make off on a straight course, in order to gain on the hunting vessels.

e) Accelerate your speed when the enemy accelerates his (or when depth charges are detonated); stop or crawl when the enemy stops. Be cautious as regards continued cruising at speed, since the sound of the screw revolving at high velocity, like all other sounds, can be detected with the antisubmarine gear (see Section I, B III, No. 59, b).

f) If possible, make your getaway in the wake of the enemy's screw, because the enemy's reception is impaired ("screened") by the disturbance caused by his own screw.

g) In narrow coastal waters (narrow bays, etc.), it is advisable to go in close to the coast, so as to stand between the enemy's ASDIC gear and the coast (deflection and multiplication of the echoes – see No. 57, b).

h) At distances under 300 m from the pursuing enemy, the ASDIC operations are ineffective, because, owing to the short distance, they give practically no results.

[. . .]

258.) According to the observations of which the results are so far available, it seems that the enemy, in many cases, operates with a combined sound locating and deep-sea echo-sounding device. After the submarine has been reported, spotted, or otherwise detected (course of the torpedo, detonation of the torpedo) the hunters endeavor as far as possible to take an accurate D/F bearing of the submarine, probably by means of sound location equipment – for this purpose the pursuit units of the enemy stop their engines – in order afterwards to approach the submarine, continually echo sounding with the submarine detecting gear, in the direction of bearing and to locate it by simple deep-sea echo sounding.

259.) Passive behavior on the part of the submarine, consisting in continually lying on the bottom of the sea, results in a danger that the position of the submarine will be betrayed by leakages from certain parts of the body of the boat (traces of oil). Consequently, stationing oneself on the bottom should be resorted to only as a temporary expedient, as a protection against specific deep-sea echo sounding (see No. 254, b), or when the submarine has already sprung a leak.

260.) If attacked with depth charges, keep a close watch on all joints, as these easily become loose as a result of vibrations, making possible large eruptions of water.

261.) If pursued for a long time, the protection afforded by darkness must in all circumstances be used in order to escape. If, in such a case, the darkness has been missed, and if the submarine finds itself, at dawn, still followed and menaced, it may have become too late to escape, especially in seasons and areas with long hours of daylight.

262.) After having traveled for a considerable length of time at great depth, on going up, before surfacing, the following rules should be observed:

a) all fastenings (joints) to be eased gradually, more especially if they have been tightened on going deep down;

b) before surfacing, get the steering gear in order again, so as to be ready for an immediate emergency dive after surfacing

c) before surfacing, pump off any excess air pressure in the boat. [. . .]

263.) As a matter of principle, every submarine commander – in view of the possibility that he may one day be surrounded by enemy forces and penned in, finding himself in a hopeless position – should plan and prepare the blowing up of the submarine by the crew itself, in every detail, with regard both to the circumstances of such an emergency and the procedure to be followed. Such a possibility must be taken into consideration more especially in the case of enemy operations in *shallow* water.

264.) Preparatory measures for blowing up your own submarine.

a) Place blasting charges (petards) for the purpose of creating several big leaks in the body of the boat, in the most suitable positions (bottom valves for admission of cooling water for the diesel engines, bottom valves for admission of sea water for the torpedo bulkheads, diesel fumes exhaust pipe underneath the ceiling with the gas flaps opened).

b) Place blasting charges (petards) or H.E. cylinders in position for the effective destruction of highly secret equipment (wireless equipment, sound locator and target detecting equipment, periscopes, fire control system, etc.). If there are not enough blasting cartridges and H.E. cylinders available for this purpose, the equipment must be smashed, so that it becomes useless.

c) Destroy secret documents of special importance by acid treatment; tie the other secret documents in a bundle, especially all wireless code data, and weight the bundles sufficiently with iron parts, for throwing overboard after surfacing.

d) Expose secret parts and mechanisms of weapons, which, when the submarine is abandoned, must be separately thrown overboard (combat pistols, etc.)

e) Prepare a brief wireless message, in order to be able to report to Headquarters the destruction by yourself of the submarine, if it should still be possible to surface.

f) After the submarine has surfaced for the last time, open the diesel head and foot valves, and empty all the compressed air tanks via the discharge valves.

265.) If it becomes necessary to blow up the boat in close proximity to the pursuing enemy, and if the position of the submarine makes it at all possible, the commander should at this moment still be concerned chiefly with the possibilities of hurting and destroying the enemy, and should use his last weapons to try to fight him.

Then the enemy covering forces should be kept in check with all available means (gun, machine gun, tommy guns, etc.), until all measures for the effective destruction of the submarine have been taken.

C. What to do in Case of Enemy Air Activity.

[. . .]

In areas specially threatened by enemy air activity; the lookout should always be taken by the best members of the crew, the A.A. weapons should be ready for action, and manned, and the serviceability of the weapons should be ensured by frequent replacement and trials (firing tests).

267.) On passage, the safety of the boat is the chief consideration during operations, the attack. On passage, the submarine should therefore dive as

A German submariner cries out for rescue after the sinking of his submarine by US naval forces.

soon as it is known that the enemy planes are trying to locate it (by radar or visual search; when attacking, it should not allow itself to be diverted from its purpose to every reconnaissance operation of enemy planes.

268.) Enemy planes which have located the submarine by radar or visual search, attack, wherever possible, out of the sun, or on the course of the submarine or the direction of diving, and turn on their headlights at night shortly before attacking.

269.) Fundamental rules: When an aircraft not flying in the direction of the submarine is sighted in the distance, do not in general submerge, but turn away, show the narrow outline, and reduce speed, so that the line of foam in the wake of the submarine disappears.

If an aircraft sighted in the distance is flying toward the submarine, submerge at once.

If a plane is sighted at night only when its lights go on in flying over, or passing near the submarine, so that it must make another run in order to attack, the submarine should submerge immediately.

If an aircraft flying toward the submarine is sighted so late that the submarine cannot get down in time, do not submerge, but fight off the plane with A.A. weapons. After the first attack, submerge at once, before the plane can make another run.

270.) After submerging during an attack, always go down at Once to depth A, and double.

SOURCES

CHAPTER 1: TRAINING AND CREW ROLES

His Majesty's Submarines (HMSO, 1945)

Submarine Information and Instruction Manual (US Submarine Division 41, Submarine Training Unit, 1942)

The Fleet Type Submarine, Navpers 16160 (Bureau of Naval Personnel, 1946)

CHAPTER 2: MAINTENANCE, DRILLS AND ROUTINES

Submarine Information and Instruction Manual (US Submarine Division 41, Submarine Training Unit, 1942)

The Fleet Type Submarine, Navpers 16160 (Bureau of Naval Personnel, 1946)

US Navy Torpedo Mark 18 (Electric): Description, Adjustment, Care, and Operation (US Navy, 1943)

CHAPTER 3: OPERATIONAL TECHNOLOGIES AND PROCEDURES

Submarine Sonar Operator's Manual, Navpers 16167 (Bureau of Naval Personnel, June 1944)

Submarine Trim and Drain Systems, Navpers 16166 (Bureau of Naval Personnel, 1946)

Standard Submarine Phraseology (Commander Submarines, Atlantic Fleet, c. 1943)

CHAPTER 4: OFFENSIVE ACTIONS – TORPEDO AND GUNNERY ATTACKS

U-boat Commander's Handbook (Department of the Navy, 1943)

CHAPTER 5: DEFENSIVE ACTIONS

The Fleet Type Submarine, Navpers 16160 (Bureau of Naval Personnel, 1946)

U-boat Commander's Handbook (Department of the Navy, 1943)